PREACHING
TO
AMERICA

PREACHING TO AMERICA

DR. LEE ROBERSON

Pastor Emeritus of the
Highland Park Baptist Church
Chattanooga, Tennessee

Chancellor of
Tennessee Temple University

SWORD of the LORD
PUBLISHERS
P. O. BOX 1099, MURFREESBORO, TN 37133

Printed and Bound in the United States of America

CONTENTS

PREFACE

I have had two purposes in my entire ministry of seventy-one years.

My first purpose has been to win souls. Without Christ, men are lost and Hell-bound. I have wanted to tell them that the only way of salvation is trusting in the Lord Jesus Christ as their Saviour. As a result, I have had the joy of seeing thousands saved.

The second purpose of my ministry has been to help Christians grow in grace and become mature, worthwhile servants of our Lord. In my pastorates, I have watched many "babes in Christ" become useful, happy Christians. In addition to the work of the Highland Park Baptist Church in Chattanooga, we established Tennessee Temple Schools in 1946 for the purpose of teaching and training men and women to be useful servants of the Lord.

In my ministry in hundreds of churches in all parts of America and in many foreign lands, I have maintained my dual purpose: to win souls and to train Christians for useful service.

INTRODUCTION

I was eighteen years old, timid and fearful, when I preached my first sermon in a small country church outside of Jeffersontown, Kentucky. I had typed the message on green typing paper and had planned to read it, but a strong breeze through an open window scattered the pages on the floor of the little chapel, and I was left with only the Bible before me.

I struggled through a few sentences, then quickly pronounced the benediction.

That was my beginning seventy-one years ago.

My heart is overwhelmed with gratitude for the blessings of God through all these years. I pray that the message of this book will challenge, bless and encourage many hearts.

THE RIGHT MEDICINE FOR AMERICA

"Righteousness exalteth a nation: but sin is a reproach to any people."—Prov. 14:34.

"But as for me and my house, we will serve the Lord."—Josh. 24:15.

"For the wages of sin is death; but the gift of God is eternal life through Jesus Christ our Lord."—Rom. 6:23.

"Wherefore, if meat make my brother to offend, I will eat no flesh while the world standeth, lest I make my brother to offend."—I Cor. 8:13.

My dear friends, America is sick! She is sinsick! We see it everywhere—in every city, every village, every state. It is revealed in the actions in Washington, D.C., in the Congress and in all of the offices. The conduct of our nation reveals the sickness—a nation turned to immorality, homosexuality, robbery, murder, and on and on.

In Washington, D.C. in one year there were 383 murders—in one year in our capital! America is sick!

Broken homes are everywhere. Half of the marriages end in divorce. In the past thirty years there have been 47 million divorces, believe it or not! At the same time, 18 million babies were killed by abortion. The Associated Press reported 80,000 cases of child abuse in Georgia in one year.

The state Family and Children Services said they were beaten, raped, starved, burned, and it went on to mention many things that had happened to these 80,000 children in *one* state.

America is sick! This is revealed in our churches. Between 3,500 and 4,000 churches close their doors every year. We have fewer churches now than we had twenty years ago. Seven thousand Southern Baptist churches did not have a single baptism during one recent year. Yes, I said seven thousand. They had churches, buildings, pastors, but no one baptized. That same year over four hundred churches took the bankruptcy law.

America is sick! This is revealed in our educational program. The Bible and prayer are out! Licentiousness and sexual freedom are in our schools. We are failing. Listen to this: The Children's Defense Fund reports that during every twenty-four-hour period in the United States, 437 teens are arrested for drunk driving, 1,206 unwed teens have abortions, 1,365 unwed teens give birth, 11,512 teens drop out of school, 3,288 teens are runaways from home, and 135,000 teens carry guns to school.

America is sick! Floods will not cure us. Famines, fires, wars and depression fail to awaken us.

The right medicine is not in laws, not in police, not in penitentiaries, not in education, not in hospitals, not in companies or groups.

"The Right Medicine for America." I got the title from a newspaper while preaching in Hartford, Connecticut. The article talked about two pharmaceutical organizations and about medicine. As I thought of that title, it spoke to my heart. America is sick! We are sinsick! *Where* is the right medicine? *What* is the right medicine? What do we need in this country? And what will do us the most good in this hour?

I. THE WORD OF GOD IS
THE RIGHT MEDICINE

I hold in my hands the world's greatest Book. I am told that in the public library in New York City there are more than one hundred million volumes. But this Book, this Bible, is worth more than them all. The Bible is God's eternal Word. Here is the right answer for all, whether on Wall Street, New York or in Washington, D.C. or Possum Trot, Tennessee. "All scripture is given by inspiration of God" (II Tim. 3:16).

Since I retired in 1983, I have preached in over 1,800 churches—an average of 118 meetings a year. I have found that most people have never read the Bible through.

In Michigan, a man walked down the aisle in tears. He said he had been the pastor of a certain church for nine years. "I have never read the Bible from cover to cover," he confessed. He named books he had never read and said, "I read my text, prepare my sermon and preach it, and that is all."

The Word of God is what our nation needs and what each individual needs. It is the right medicine to cure our ills.

Some folks are like the boy in Memphis, Tennessee who came up to me and said, "Brother Roberson, will you sign my Bible?" I took the beautiful new Bible, opened it and signed my name, handed it back and said, "Now, son, be sure to read it."

He immediately said, "Oh, I don't read the Bible. I have a whole wall full of new Bibles, all different versions. I just collect them."

I know a lot of folks like him. They have a Bible but don't read it. Get back in the Bible!

Some people are like the lady I was visiting in Chattanooga. She was up in years. When I came to the end of my visit, I said, "I would like to read some verses from your Bible and have prayer with you."

She got up, went over and opened the bottom drawer of a dresser, took out a box, got out her brand-new Bible and said, "I take care of my Bible. I don't want it to get dirty or soiled or torn, so I put it away."

When I opened it and read from it, I saw that she had not been reading it.

Read the Word. Believe the Word. Obey the Word. Defend the Bible against critics. Preach the Word of God.

Sunday school teachers, what power and influence you have! I was led to Christ by a lady Sunday school teacher when I was fourteen. She taught a big class of roughneck boys. She began every class by giving the way of salvation, and I got saved.

Teachers, keep at it night and day. Build your class. Don't give up.

I go to churches where they have fifty or fewer in Sunday school. I want to help them if I can. But for years they stay the same in numbers. They are not growing.

In these meetings I mention four things:

1. Reach adults. Go after men and women. Build large, strong adult classes. Get the people in. Organize the class. Give it a name (Joy, Grace, Victory, etc.). Have officers, group captains. Go after the adults. These bring kids with them. These bring in the money. These give to missions and to other Christian works.

2. Take a survey. Let me recommend that you do this in your churches. I know what it means, because I did it in Chattanooga. Carlyle Brooks spent six months covering the city—150 houses a day. We got names of unsaved people, and I wrote them letters once a month.

I tell preachers, "Write letters." You can make copies, but sign them personally. Simply tell them you are the pastor of a certain church, and offer nothing but your services to them. Tell them to call on you if you can help them in any way. Give your telephone number.

If you send a letter each month, sooner or later people are going to start calling. They want help and you can help them. When you are invited to come to their home, that gives you the opportunity to witness to them and win them.

Go after people. Seek to reach adults and win them to the Lord.

3. Increase the enrollment of your Sunday school. First, enroll your whole church in Sunday school. Every church member should be on the roll of some class. And enroll them as they join. Some churches don't do this until they come three times, but that is not the best way. And don't take them off the roll unless they die, move out of the city or join another church.

Use buses and vans to bring in people who need transportation.

II. SURRENDER TO THE WILL OF GOD

The right medicine for America is a surrender to the will of God. I believe that God has a will for every man, woman and child. But even Christians, including preachers, ignore the will of God.

I just read a two-page letter today written by a graduate of our school. He had preached twenty years and was a successful pastor. Then he got caught up with a woman of the church and gave up the ministry altogether. Now he is miserable. He comes back to see his wife once in awhile, but he is so unhappy out of the will of God.

God has a will for us individually and as a nation. We suffer for it when we get out of that will.

I was pastor at Highland Park Baptist Church for forty years and six months. Then I felt led of God to retire. I simply knew it was God's will. I offered my resignation at almost seventy-four years of age. I told my people that God had led me.

You must stay in the will of God no matter what people

say or do or what your family thinks. His will brings peace
and happiness and usefulness.

We tell more falsehoods in church than anywhere else.
You sing "Have Thine Own Way, Lord," but half of you do
not mean it. Many don't tithe, don't come to church when
you should, don't pray, don't read the Bible. Don't sing a lie!
Mean it when you sing "Have Thine Own Way, Lord."

This conference can be the greatest thing ever to happen
to you. After listening to these great preachers, you can go
away determined to do the will of God.

In your church, in your Sunday school class, in your
youth work, do you want the will of God to be done?

I was called to preach at the age of eighteen, then started to
pastor churches in Memphis, Tennessee, then at Greenbrier,
Tennessee. At Greenbrier I was paid $75.00 a month. The
church built me a little room on the back out of secondhand
lumber. There was no running water, no bathroom.

I lived three years in a bare room in a little country
church on the outside of town. I had no cooking facilities. I
would visit my church folks at noontime every day! I had
finished the university at Louisville, my hometown, and had
been to the Southern Baptist Seminary. And here I was in
this little room!

I had studied a lot of music and had been singing all my
life. I got a job at WSM in Nashville, where I sang every week
and got paid for it! I also sang for WSIX in Springfield,
Tennessee. I liked it. I got to thinking that I might be able to
do something with this.

I went to the Nashville Conservatory and saw the man in
charge. I told him I wanted him to hear me sing. I told him
what I was doing on the radio.

I sang two songs. When I finished, he walked out of the
room, was gone a little while, walked back in with a sheet of
paper in his hand and said, "I like it. I will take you. I can

do something for you. I will give you lessons."

He said he had only done this once before, but he wanted to train me and put me in the big stuff—I mean BIG stuff! He mentioned names of those I knew about in that day that I would be working with. He said he would give me five lessons a week and get me a job in Nashville to pay my expenses and so on. He said he had a contract in his hand that he wanted me to sign.

I was excited about what he had said, about taking lessons from this great teacher and about what was ahead, about the money I would be getting. (I was living on $75.00 a month.)

I took the pen in hand and was ready to sign. Then I read what was written, agreeing to let him arrange all of the meetings and engagements for singing. I said, "Sir, what does that mean?"

He said, "Just what it says. You sing when I say sing, and you do what I say or tell you to do. We will keep this rule in effect for a year while I am training you. Just sign the paper."

I told him then that I was pastor of a little country church and preached on Sunday morning, Sunday night and Wednesday night; that I led singing in all of the services and sang all the solos.

He said, "Well, give it up. Turn your back on that. You do what I say, and I will guarantee you big money—thousands a year, maybe $150,000 a year. Just sign the paper."

Then, all of a sudden, I realized that God had called me to preach, called me to a ministry. So I said, "Sir, I appreciate your kindness, but I cannot sign that paper because I plan to keep on preaching." And I handed that contract back to him.

I can still see that hot-headed Italian as he took that paper, looked at it and said, "You mean you won't take what

I'm offering you? Remember, you are only the second man I have ever given that offer."

I said, "I'm sorry, but I can't sign it."

He took that paper, tore it into little shreds, dropped it on the floor and began to curse me.

I walked out, got in my old Chevrolet and drove up Church Street, right in the center of Nashville, the happiest man in the world—happy because I had said "yes" to the Lord and to His will. I have never had to fight that battle again!

Wait a minute! You do what I did—surrender your life to the Lord.

Some things you don't have to argue about. Gambling is not the will of God. Drunkenness is not the will of God. Immorality is not the will of God. Carelessness is not His will. Rebellion is not in His will. Indifference is not in God's will. When you determine to do the will of God, that changes everything.

So many men jump up and want to quit. I suppose I get at least one phone call a week, maybe more, from preachers ready to quit the ministry because things didn't go right.

The right medicine for you is to surrender to the will of God.

III. RETURN TO THE WORK OF GOD

I have spoken here of the Word of God and the will of God. Now I speak of the work of God—doing what God says. This means:

1. Return to prayer. Prayer is work. The Devil fights you when you go to pray. He disturbs and distracts you. He does all he can to keep you from praying. But you determine to pray and seek the face of God, to wait on Him.

Prayer can make your trying days triumphant days. Begin your day with prayer.

I cannot forget, when I mention prayer, Dr. John R. Rice. Oh, how he prayed!

We were in a meeting in Monroe, Louisiana. I preached Monday morning; he preached Monday night. Tuesday morning I got up at 6:00 o'clock, went out and got my breakfast and came back to the room.

A knock came at my door about 6:45. There stood Dr. Rice, holding that red Scofield Bible he always carried. He said, "Brother Roberson, may I come in? Could we pray together?"

I said, "Yes sirree."

He came in, sat down, and we read four or five chapters from the Bible. Then he said, "Let's pray. I will pray first and then you pray."

I got down by his side, and he began to pray for his wife, children and grandchildren, every employee of the Sword, calling all by name. Then he began to pray for preachers— some two hundred—by name! I never heard anything like it! Then he prayed for some of his enemies, some who were fighting him.

Fifteen minutes went by, twenty, then twenty-five minutes. I was still by his side getting ready to pray. He was still pouring out his heart, talking to God. He went on calling people by name to the Lord.

Then he stopped and said, "O Brother Roberson, excuse me, please. I forgot you were here. Now, will you pray?"

I said, "Dr. Rice, excuse me; I don't feel like praying." And I didn't. You know why? He had already covered the ground, and I had prayed with him.

Dr. Rice taught me something about prayer. He didn't have to, but that was his custom, to pray for definite people by name every day.

Listen. That is work! When we are too busy to pray, we are *too* busy.

2. Return to worship. Even some great men, good men, need this. I am a bit disturbed that some preachers are slack in going to church. Some can take a vacation and skip church altogether. Or they take a trip overseas and don't go to church. Don't neglect God's house. It is medicine for your soul. Go Sunday morning, Sunday night and Wednesday night. "Three to Thrive" is my motto. Urge your people to attend all services faithfully.

What would happen if the president of the United States would go on television at 7:00 o'clock every morning, read a whole chapter from the Bible and offer a prayer, covering about fifteen minutes, then close by saying, "I am urging the people of my nation to be in church every Sunday morning, every Sunday night, and attend prayer meeting Wednesday night"?

You might think, *Why, the president can't do that.* Yes, he can. He can command his time.

I predict that we could settle ninety percent of all our problems in this country if we would just put God first.

A return to worship, to the house of God, is the right medicine.

3. Return to compassion. The right medicine is a concern for others around us.

The right medicine in America is a recognition of our sin, a repentance of our sin, a return to godliness, a return to prayer, to soul winning, to witnessing, to compassion.

A nation may not do it, but I can do it, and you can do it. When we do, it will show in the church.

I am here today because of a Sunday school teacher named Mrs. Daisy Hawes who led me to Christ. You are here because someone led you to Jesus. Not one in this building can say, "No one helped me. I got saved all by myself." No, God uses people. Someone gave you a Bible or a gospel tract, or you heard the Gospel preached on radio or television. We are all here because someone cared. By compassion, we came to Christ.

We ran thirty-five buses at our church, but we began with one. A man named M. J. Parker came into the church. He had snow-white hair, though in his fifties. He got saved. I baptized him and his wife. He began working in the church. He came to me and said, "Let's buy a bus. Let's try it." (No one in Chattanooga had ever tried it.)

So we bought a bus. Though he had a full-time job with National Linen Company, he said he would give as much time to the bus route as he could. Soon he filled it up.

We bought a second bus, then a third one, and on and on until we owned thirty-five. All would come into the parking lot packed every Sunday morning, Sunday night and Wednesday night.

Dr. Clarence Sexton came in and worked with us after Brother Parker passed away. For five years Dr. Sexton did an amazing work. Thousands were saved through the ministry that he led.

Oh, that we had more men and women like that—sold out to God! Brother Parker didn't finish the third grade in school, but he became a mighty soul winner because of his concern and compassion.

The right medicine for America is not money, bigger hospitals, more jails or penitentiaries, more recreation, more highly paid teachers in public or private schools; but a concern, a compassion. Our churches, our cities, our towns and villages, our nation and the world need the right medicine.

We talked about the Word of God, the will of God, the work of God—the right medicine for America.

I am eighty-nine, will be ninety in November. Before God takes me Home, I want to do all I can for my Lord and for people around me. I want to use every opportunity to point people to the Lamb of God.

If you are lost, come to Jesus and receive Him now. If you want the Lord to use your life in every way, please come in complete surrender to Him.

I was in a tent meeting in front of the Concord Baptist Church at Birmingham, Alabama. The tent was full. I was facing the big main highway. A man on a motorcycle came by. He slowed down as he got in front of the tent and shouted, "Hallelujah! Praise God! Amen!" I saw people shudder. Some bowed their heads in embarrassment, while others didn't even turn around, seemingly knowing who this was.

I was reading the Scriptures, and I kept right on. The man went up the road about a mile, turned around and came back at full speed, slowed down and shouted the same words again. The people reacted the same, but I went on preaching, then gave the invitation.

From the second or third row came a man, a woman and a young lady. I jumped off the platform and met them. "Why have you come?"

They answered, "We want to be saved."

I took my Bible and led them to the Lord. I had them stand at the front so people could come by and shake hands and rejoice with them.

Someone walked up to me and asked, "Do you know who they are?"

I said, "No."

"They are the father, the mother and the sister of the boy on the motorcycle who rode by and shouted."

I said, "Tomorrow I will see that boy."

Before I left the tent, the pastor asked if I had heard that this was the family of the boy. Then he said he wanted to go see him the next day. When I told him I had decided to see him myself, he said, "You are the evangelist. I am the pastor. It is my place to see him. I will see him as I visit the family about being baptized and coming into the church."

But he did not get to see him the next day. The young man on the motorcycle rode back into Birmingham, out the highway going toward Tuscaloosa; and between Bessemer and Tuscaloosa, past the midnight hour, he drove into a tree and was killed instantly.

The word came to me and the pastor. We both wanted to talk with him; now he was gone. When I told the pastor I would be praying for him as he talked with the family, he said, "You will have to go. I can't go down there."

I told him he was the one to go—he was the pastor; I was just the evangelist. But he insisted he couldn't go.

So I went down to a big, white, two-story farmhouse. The door was open, so I went in. Seeing the casket at the far end of the living room, I went over and looked into the face of that boy who, just a few hours ago, had ridden down the highway shouting, "Hallelujah! Praise the Lord! Amen!" in a mocking way.

The door opened from the back of the home, and the father came in. Crying, he grabbed my arm and said he had lost the best friend he ever had. He talked about how close they were and how much he loved him.

Then the mother appeared. She grabbed my other arm and told me how sweet the boy was to her and what a good time they had had together.

Remember, she, her husband and daughter had just been saved the night before, and their loved one was lying there in death.

The sister came then, walked up to the casket and touched him and patted him and cried.

Now, what do you say to a family who has lost their loved one suddenly like this? I said, "Folks, let's pray and ask God to help us." I tried to pray. I didn't do very well, but I tried.

When I had finished praying, this new convert, the

father, said, "Brother Roberson, would you mind letting us use your tent for the funeral?"

I said, "You can use it."

The funeral was on Sunday afternoon. The tent was packed and overflowing—more than two thousand people attended. The preacher gave a message, then the invitation. Many came forward to accept Christ as Saviour.

I came back on Sunday night to the same tent to preach, and God blessed that service. At the end, the preacher walked up to me with hands outstretched and asked me to look at them, saying, "Do you see it, Brother Roberson?"

"No, I don't," I said.

"I have bloody hands. Do you know where I live? Right down the road from where these people live, and just five miles from church. When I go to and from church, I drive right by their home. For five long years I have gone by their home every day or a couple of times a day and told myself, *I must stop and see those folks.* But in five years I never stopped once. I knew they were lost. And I said I would stop someday, but I never did. Now I have bloody hands!"

I responded, "You are right." He had failed to warn the wicked (Ezek. 33:8).

We too shall have bloody hands if we fail to warn the wicked, fail to preach the Gospel, fail to tell people of Christ, the loving Saviour.

Whatever others may do, tell God you want His will done. Come back to the Word of God; come back to the will of God; and come back to the work of God.

2
THE LIGHT OF THE WORLD

"Ye are the light of the world. A city that is set on an hill cannot be hid.

"Neither do men light a candle, and put it under a bushel, but on a candlestick; and it giveth light unto all that are in the house.

"Let your light so shine before men, that they may see your good works, and glorify your Father which is in heaven."—Matt. 5:14–16.

"But ye, brethren, are not in darkness, that that day should overtake you as a thief.

"Ye are all the children of light, and the children of the day: we are not of the night, nor of darkness.

"Therefore let us not sleep, as do others; but let us watch and be sober.

"For they that sleep sleep in the night; and they that be drunken are drunken in the night.

"But let us, who are of the day, be sober, putting on the breastplate of faith and love; and for an helmet, the hope of salvation.

"For God hath not appointed us to wrath, but to obtain salvation by our Lord Jesus Christ,

"Who died for us, that, whether we wake or sleep, we should live together with him."—I Thess. 5:4–10.

Jesus said, "Ye are the light of the world." Every Christian is to shine and be a light for the Lord. If you are

saved, then you are to shine; you are to let it be known
that you belong to the Lord. We are to shine. We are every
day to give glory to God, to praise Him, to let our life shine.

Robert Louis Stevenson told the story of a little boy looking out a window and watching the men come down the
street lighting lights in the old lampstands. Every night he
watched them climb a ladder, light the lamp, then move on
to the next one.

When asked what he was doing, he replied, "I'm watching
the men knock holes in the darkness."

This world is in darkness, in sin, and we are to shine and
"knock holes in the darkness."

At one time sixty-four percent of the population of
America had church membership. Today that figure is less
than forty percent. In 1900 there were twenty-seven
churches for every ten thousand Americans. In 1985 there
were only twelve churches for every ten thousand Americans.

Between 3,500 and 4,000 churches, counting all denomi-
nations in our country, close their doors every year. In a
recent year, 400 churches took bankruptcy. Some 7,000
Southern Baptist churches had pastors, buildings and
programs, but not one person was saved and baptized in
a full year.

In America, there are 21,500 women preachers—900 of
them Southern Baptists. I am pointing out the need of
this day and the darkness of the world. We are to live every
day for the Lord, giving forth a definite, positive testimony
for Christ.

We are to "knock holes in the darkness."

I. BY THE WAY WE LIVE

"None of us liveth to himself, and no man dieth to himself." Do we live so people know we belong to the Lord?
Something is wrong if the people among whom we live are

not sure we are saved. The way we live is very important.

In a meeting in Birmingham, Alabama, the pastor said just a few moments before the service, "Brother Roberson, let's get in the car and drive to Five Points. I want you to talk to an unsaved man whom I have been trying to win to the Lord. His wife belongs to our church."

We got in the car and went to the apartment. The pastor rang the doorbell. He introduced the man's wife to me and told her why we were there.

She took us to see her husband. I shook his hand and said, "We don't have much time, but I want to ask you if you are a Christian."

He said, "No."

When I told him that he needed to be, he seemed rather unconcerned. I read to him clearly the way of salvation, then prayed with him. Then I asked him if he would trust the Lord.

He said, "No, no. It doesn't mean a thing to me."

I didn't want to give up, so I read some more. When I wanted to pray with him again, he said he was not interested. Nevertheless, I asked him to kneel with me in prayer.

I began praying. All of a sudden I heard a thumping noise, something hitting the floor, and some wailing. I couldn't help it—I looked. Over by the window the wife had dropped out of her chair and was beating the floor, praying, "Lord, if he goes to Hell, it is my fault!" She had been compromising with the Devil. She was saved but not living for Christ, not letting her light shine. She knew it, and he knew it.

While she was crying and beating the floor, I stopped praying and looked at her. I turned back to the man, and, lo and behold, he was crying!

I said, "Sir, do you want to be saved?"

"Yes sir, right now."

I led that man to the Lord. He stood to his feet, wiped away the tears and said, "Thank you, Preacher. I have been wanting this for a long time."

I said, "God bless you! Come to church next Sunday and come down the aisle."

He said, "Next Sunday? I am coming tonight!"

We had a revival meeting going on. He did come that night, and he came forward. I saw him later get baptized. Today he is living for Christ.

What am I saying? When the wife got right with the Lord, her husband got saved. See the importance of our living for the Lord, separated from the world?

Be faithful in all services of your church. Be faithful in your giving. Glorify God in your living. Receive peace of mind by your unity in Christ. Do these, then you will get your prayers answered.

II. BY THE TESTIMONY OF OUR LIPS

"But ye shall receive power, after that the Holy Ghost is come upon you: and ye shall be witnesses unto me both in Jerusalem, and in all Judæa, and in Samaria, and unto the uttermost part of the earth."—Acts 1:8.

We will "knock holes in the darkness" every time we witness for Christ. We cause people to think of God, of Christ, of salvation, of life everlasting, of a life in Hell without Christ.

I used to go quite often to Charleston, West Virginia to speak in the old rescue mission which Pat Withral operated. Pat, a great fellow, would always meet me at the airport. A mission man would drive the car while we sat in the back seat. As we came down the hill from the airport, Pat would always say to the driver, "Tell Brother Roberson what happened to you." And the driver would testify of his faith in Jesus Christ and tell about his getting saved.

When I asked Pat later why he always asked the driver

to tell what happened to him, he said, "Brother Roberson, I found out something. If a man will keep close to the Lord and keep on witnessing, God will bless him."

Keep witnessing. Keep telling what Jesus did for you.

This is my second thought—we should "knock holes in the darkness" by the testimony of our lips. "Ye shall be witnesses unto me." Tell about Christ the Saviour everywhere you go.

One Sunday morning a young man was saved at Highland Park Baptist Church. He wanted to be baptized, and I baptized him. When I brought him up out of the water, he said, "Brother Roberson, pray for my wife. She is lost." I told him I would. I asked if I could come and see her that very afternoon. He said, "No, no. I want to talk to her myself. I just got saved, and I know what happened to me." That was pretty smart, wasn't it? I told him to go right ahead. We had prayer and he left.

Sunday night the auditorium was filled—balcony and downstairs—with chairs set up in the aisles. I looked for my man. Finally I saw him in the back on the last row. I could not miss this tall man. Not seeing anyone with him, I assumed he didn't get results that afternoon while talking with his wife. I supposed he would now ask me to come by and see her.

I preached the sermon, gave the invitation, and he was the first down the aisle. Then I saw this short woman with him. He came right to me, introduced his wife and said, "I led her to Christ this afternoon." I questioned her, and she seemed very sure of her salvation. That night I had the joy of baptizing her.

God will use us if we are surrendered and usable.

III. BY OUR VISION

"Where there is no vision, the people perish" (Prov. 29:18). In Matthew 9:36 Jesus saw the multitudes and had compassion on them. We are to "knock holes in the darkness" by our vision of a lost and dying world.

I believe that without Christ, people are lost and will spend eternity in Hell. It matters not what country they live in—America, Africa, Japan, Spain—we have a job to do. We should give our money, time and energy. Tell the Lord, "I want to 'knock holes in the darkness' by a vision of this lost world. Give me that vision!"

We had a faithful lady in our church, Miss Frances Woods—I can still see her. She was the head nurse at Campbell's Clinic. One Sunday morning she came forward and said, "God has called me to go to Africa as a missionary."

I was shocked. She was beyond the age that some mission boards would accept. I talked with her. She still insisted that she was going.

She enrolled in Tennessee Temple, took Bible training, then was sent out by the Southern Rhodesia Mission.

Later, this tremendous missionary came home and gave her testimony. I will never forget it.

When she went back after one of her furloughs, she met a young man named Michael Warburton. This tall Englishman, an engineer, had gone into Africa on a project, and they met and fell in love. They served God together— she as a missionary and he as an engineer.

They lived in a little grass hut outside the mission compound. One morning she prepared breakfast and called him. But when he didn't respond, she went into the bedroom. He said, "Honey, I can't move. I'm paralyzed. My legs won't move."

Being a nurse, she knew what to do. After working on him a bit, she sent for a doctor. Her husband was put in the hospital. He was paralyzed from the waist down. We heard all about it by letters coming from the field.

They decided to come to America—he had never been

here before. We got them a place to stay next to our house on Bailey Avenue. This very dignified, highly educated Englishman was in a wheelchair. They came faithfully to church.

One morning while I was walking down Orchard Knob Avenue, I saw him coming toward me at a fast pace in his wheelchair. He rolled right up to me and stopped, all excited. "Preacher, I must tell you something exciting. God has just called me to be a missionary!"

I said, "Mike, that's wonderful! But of course, it will be a little difficult with you paralyzed."

He said, "You didn't hear me, did you? God has called me to be a missionary."

I said, "I believe I did hear you."

He said, "I am going back to the field after I raise my support." He raised his support and went. He is there right now serving God and building churches. He invented a little automobile that he can drive with his hands. He goes from church to church, preaching and winning souls. He is paralyzed, yet he does all of that!

We are to "knock holes in the darkness" by our vision of a lost and dying world—give our money, give our children, give ourselves—give our all to the Lord!

Get a vision of your local field. Literally thousands of lost people are all around you, and hundreds of thousands within a few miles. Get a vision of your field.

God gave me and my wife a very beautiful little baby girl. We named her Joy, for she brought such joy to our hearts. We were very happy. After a few months she suddenly became ill and passed away. The death of our baby broke our hearts. We didn't try to understand it. We just said, "Lord, Your will be done."

One day God told me He wanted to use the death of our little one to help others. God led me to start Camp Joy for children in memory of our little one. We had no land, so I prayed, and the TVA put up one hundred acres for sale at Lake Chickamauga. I went to the auction at the courthouse. Hundreds were there. People wanted that land. The auctioneer said the land was worth three or four hundred thousand dollars, maybe five hundred thousand. It was valuable land, close to the lake, and a beautiful piece of property.

I was sitting in the back of the room, my heart pressed with the matter of a camp, getting land where we could give children the Gospel. I wanted the poor and forgotten ones to be able to go to camp. I kept praying.

After awhile the auctioneer said, "Well, what am I bid?"

I don't know why in the world I said it, but I stood up and said, "Sir, I bid three thousand dollars." He laughed. The crowd laughed. I sat down. I prayed.

The auctioneer said, "Thank you, sir, but this land is valuable property and worth a hundred times what you offered." Then he said, "Now, we will continue the bidding," ignoring me altogether.

You know who got the property? I did! You know how much I paid? Three thousand dollars!

After it was all over, I walked up to him and said, "Sir, I am the man who bought the property."

"Yes, I know you are. And how did you do that?"

I said, "I can't explain it, except the Lord showed me what to do. I am going to build a camp up there for children." Then I said, "But, sir, I am embarrassed. I don't have three thousand dollars."

He said, "You don't have the money?"

"No sir. I don't have a nickel right now. But if you will give me twenty-four hours, you will have it in hand."

I went out and raised the money and paid him the next day!

The camp has now been going since 1946. We have taken

thousands of children there to hear the Gospel. The poor and forgotten children can go to camp free. Many missionaries, pastors and other Christian workers have come out of that crowd.

Get a vision of your local field and what God can use you to do there. Then get a vision of an individual's need. Your dearest loved ones are lost without Christ. Tell God you will do all you can to bring them to the Saviour.

"Knock holes in the darkness." Live every day so someone can see Christ in you. Cause others to want what you have.

Saved by the grace of God and the blood of Christ! Are you saved? If not, ask Jesus Christ now to forgive your sins and trust Him as your Saviour.

.

THE STERN DISCIPLINE OF LIFE

"But put ye on the Lord Jesus Christ, and make not provision for the flesh, to fulfil the lusts thereof."—Rom. 13:14.

"But now I have written unto you not to keep company, if any man that is called a brother be a fornicator, or covetous, or an idolater, or a railer, or a drunkard, or an extortioner; with such an one no not to eat."—I Cor. 5:11.

"But I keep under my body, and bring it into subjection: lest that by any means, when I have preached to others, I myself should be a castaway."—I Cor. 9:27.

A Christian magazine carried the following story:

Mr. Cecil one day went into a room where his little black-eyed girl was, happy as she could be. Someone had just given her a box of beautiful beads. She went to her father immediately to show this little gift.

"They are very beautiful, my child," he said; "but now, my dear, throw them into the fire.

"Now I shall not compel you to do so; I leave it to you. But you never knew Daddy to ask you to do a thing that was not kind to you. I cannot tell you why, but if you can trust me, do so."

It cost a great effort, but the little one began, in her own way, to think, *Father has always been kind to me. I suppose he is right.* So she took the box and with a great effort, threw it into the fire.

Her father said no more for some time.

The next day, however, he gave her something far more beautiful, something she had long desired.

"Now, my child," said he, "I did this to teach you to trust in that greater Father in Heaven. Many times in life He will require you to give up something and avoid what you cannot see the reasons for avoiding; but if you trust Him, you will always find it best."

That story gives a beginning to this message. Paul maintained stern discipline. He knew he was saved by grace; he knew the indwelling power of the Holy Spirit, but he knew that God desired certain things from him. And to make these things real, it was necessary that Paul watch himself carefully and keep himself disciplined.

The apostle exhorted us many times to turn from sin and to walk circumspectly. The passage in Romans 13 is one of them, when he said:

"Let us walk honestly, as in the day; not in rioting and drunkenness, not in chambering and wantonness, not in strife and envying.

"But put ye on the Lord Jesus Christ, and make not provision for the flesh, to fulfil the lusts thereof."—Vss. 13,14.

He gives the same kind of exhortation in I Corinthians 5. When great sin had entered the church at Corinth, the apostle exhorted them to turn away from sin and live in such a way that they would be known as the children of God. He even told them to turn away from those who be "a fornicator, or covetous, or an idolater, or a railer, or a drunkard, or an extortioner."

To simplify the message, I give an outline that you can remember. Paul had a definite discipline of self. What brought this about?

I. HIS ALLEGIANCE TO CHRIST

We shall not take the time to look into that remarkable experience on the road to Damascus, when the Lord Jesus appeared and spoke to Saul. We believe this was when Paul met Christ and was saved.

Paul had hated Christ and Christians. He was then on his way to Damascus to bring to prison any who followed after the Saviour. But now his hate had turned to love.

But notice also that Paul's love turned to hate. He had loved the bitter way, the antagonistic way, the anti-Christ way. Now his love turned to hate. He hated the sinful way, the way of his past. Now he loved Christ.

The Bible is such an amazing Book! For example, Acts, chapter 8, gives the conversion of the Ethiopian eunuch. Philip led this one to the Lord Jesus Christ. In Acts 9 is the conversion of Saul of Tarsus. What a contrast between the two men and the two conversions!

The eunuch quietly, thoughtfully, deliberately accepted Christ. He had been giving consideration to this matter. As he traveled, he was reading Isaiah 53; now when Philip came to him, he at once turned to Christ and received Him.

The conversion of Saul was as a flash of a meteor. What a mighty, unusual experience came to him as he traveled the road to Damascus! It took the unusual to bring this man about-face and to the Saviour.

I mention these cases because we are sometimes prone to criticize the one whose salvation experience was not the same as ours. Some people believe one must come to an altar to be saved. Some have strong doubts about anyone's being saved outside the church. Others believe that salvation comes only when there are certain external actions, marks and sounds.

The important thing is to meet the Lord and to receive Him as Saviour. This Paul did!

From the time of his conversion, Paul was a devout follower of the Lord Jesus. His allegiance never changed. Suffering did not change him—and how much he suffered!

He spent much time in prison, was beaten with many stripes, was stoned. He spent hours in weariness and painfulness. Yet somehow the apostle could still rejoice. From behind prison bars in Rome, he wrote to the church in Philippi, "Rejoice in the Lord."

Someday someone will write a book on jails and prisons and what they have contributed to Christianity. He will write about Paul's imprisonments. He will tell us about John on Patmos. He will give the full story of John Bunyan. He will tell the story of Savanarola. He will tell us about Luther and his prison experiences.

Paul's sufferings did not change his allegiance.

Criticism did not change him. He heard it from his own people, the Jews. He heard it from his enemies. He even had criticism from the people in the churches, as revealed in I and II Corinthians. When they accused Paul of many things, he wrote to set them right in positive declarations of his faith.

Loneliness did not change his allegiance. Paul was often alone. He called himself on one occasion "an ambassador in bonds." There are lonely hours for those who serve Christ. Others do not always agree with us. When the world ostracizes us, we must still take our stand for Christ.

Keep in mind that I am trying to answer the question regarding Paul's stern discipline of himself. His allegiance to Christ made this obligatory.

Christ was the One who made life meaningful to Paul. Christ was the One who lived and then died on the cross, who was buried in the tomb, raised from the dead; and Paul said, "For I know whom I have believed."

This week I was reading a book written some years ago by a so-called minister. He told the story of Jesus, His death on the cross, His burial in the grave and His resurrection. Then he said, "Such is the story of Easter. Whether literal

or symbolic, this has caught the imagination of the world."
He went on to say, "I don't know that it matters whether we
believe it as a literal fact or only as symbolic beauty."

Poor, doubting man! What hope could a man like this
have? But Paul doubted not! Christ was real to him. And to
Him he gave allegiance.

II. HIS CONSCIOUSNESS OF WEAKNESS

Why did Paul have such a stern discipline of himself? The
apostle knew himself. Shortly after his conversion, he said,
"I...am not meet to be called an apostle." As time went on, he
cried out, "[I] am less than the least of all saints." Just
before his death by martyrdom, he declared, 'I am the chief
of sinners.' It seems very plain that the more Paul knew
about Christ, the less he was pleased with himself and his
spiritual state.

Paul was conscious of his weakness. Are you conscious
of yours?

Paul knew the strength and power of this world. Hear
him as he shouts forth his command to the Christians in
Ephesus:

*"Finally, my brethren, be strong in the Lord, and in the power
of his might.*

*"Put on the whole armour of God, that ye may be able to stand
against the wiles of the devil."*—Eph. 6:10, 11.

Paul knew his own inability to conquer the world. He
knew his weakness, his nothingness. It would be wise for us
to know ours too. So much self-trust and self-faith comes to
us out of books of psychology and out of modern writings on
how to be a success. We must realize that we are nothing,
that we are bound to fail if we trust in ourselves.

Paul knew the fullness of the Holy Spirit's power. Hence,
he could plead with Christians, "Be filled with the Spirit."

Now what must we say? First, know your weaknesses.

Understand that you are nothing. Preachers, deacons, Sunday school teachers, youth leaders all fail when we trust in self. Second, rely on His strength, His power. What better Scripture could I read than these words in II Corinthians 12:

"And lest I should be exalted above measure through the abundance of the revelations, there was given to me a thorn in the flesh, the messenger of Satan to buffet me, lest I should be exalted above measure.

"For this thing I besought the Lord thrice, that it might depart from me.

"And he said unto me, My grace is sufficient for thee: for my strength is made perfect in weakness. Most gladly therefore will I rather glory in my infirmities, that the power of Christ may rest upon me.

"Therefore I take pleasure in infirmities, in reproaches, in necessities, in persecutions, in distresses for Christ's sake: for when I am weak, then am I strong."—Vss. 7–10.

Paul maintained a stern discipline of himself because he was conscious of his weakness.

III. HIS DESIRE TO GLORIFY GOD

Evident on every single page of Paul's writings was his desire to glorify his Heavenly Father. And this could only be done by showing forth Christ in his life. Paul could shout out, "For to me to live is Christ, and to die is gain" (Phil. 1:21).

I suggest three ways that Paul felt he could glorify God:

First, he could glorify God by clean living. He told us, "I keep under my body, and bring it into subjection." Paul then exhorts us to be separate from the world. "Wherefore come out from among them, and be ye separate, saith the Lord, and touch not the unclean thing; and I will receive you" (II Cor. 6:17).

Second, Paul felt he could glorify God by a courageous testimony in the face of opposition. We too are called upon to give our testimony when faced with rigid opposition. Speak of Christ daily. Live for Him so others can see that you belong to Him.

"Therefore, my beloved brethren, be ye stedfast, unmoveable, always abounding in the work of the Lord, forasmuch as ye know that your labour is not in vain in the Lord."—I Cor. 15:58.

Third, Paul glorified God by a consuming passion for souls. This same passion we must have. We must yearn to see people come to our Saviour. For the Jewish people, Paul had "great heaviness and continual sorrow" in his heart (Rom. 9:2). He desired to see them brought to the Lord. His heart was aching, yearning, breaking for souls to be saved.

Thank God for your salvation and its greatness, then be concerned for others. When you have a great love for Christ, it becomes a passion to tell others of Him.

Jerry McAuley spent his life on Water Street in New York City because of his passion for the Man of Galilee. David Livingstone plunged into the depths of Africa so he could tell the story of Christ to the heathen. J. Hudson Taylor went off to China because he was gripped by a passion for the Saviour and a love for men.

Do we have this consuming passion? Do we love souls and desire to bring them to the Saviour? Someone has said, "God's pathway to one human heart is through another human heart." God uses us to bring souls to Himself. If we fail, the message does not get out.

Has winning souls become the great purpose of your life? This task is so tremendous that all other things become minute and unimportant.

Some of you may yearn to be soul winners. You would like to have a consuming passion for souls. Then perhaps I should advise you as Henry Ford advised his men: "Start where you stand."

What he meant was: There is no use to go back into past history, no use to repeat your life story. Be concerned about one thing—your work now. Therefore, he told them, "Start where you stand."

This is a good word for all of us who desire to win souls and glorify God.

A missionary tells of being in Europe in 1949. The war had just ended. Refugees were everywhere. One true story about a little boy stayed with him:

> The boy stumbled into a refugee camp. Part of one leg was shot away, so he walked with the help of an old broom. After he had walked many, many miles, that broom had worn a hole under his arm, and gangrene had set in.
>
> The nurse at the refugee camp was deeply moved as she looked at the lad. "Does it hurt?" she asked.
>
> "No," he answered.
>
> She looked into his dry, hollow eyes and queried, "It must hurt somewhere."
>
> Finally he pointed to his heart and said, "It only hurts inside."

Perhaps I can apply that story to say that we need to have a hurt in our hearts, a consuming passion for the souls of men.

This world is filled with those whose hearts are darkened by sin. They suffer from broken hearts, broken hopes and broken lives. It is our duty to go to them with broken hearts and tell the story of Jesus and how He is ready to save them.

Our invitation to you is: Will you come to the Lord Jesus Christ and receive Him as Saviour? If you have already accepted Christ, will you come and testify to your faith in Him? Whatever may be your need, God is able to meet that need. Come to Christ today!

THE HIDDEN LIFE

"For ye are dead, and your life is hid with Christ in God."—Col. 3:3.

I am constantly seeking for some "fresh" word that I can give to those who come to me seeking help. I know the Word of God has the answer for every problem. But I look for a new way to speak to that seeking, groping soul.

What do most people want?

They want the assurance of salvation. They want to know that all is well with their souls. Yes, some may seek assurance when they are not saved. What a joy to point people to Christ who saves, keeps and satisfies!

People want peace of heart. Every person has the same desire—peace of heart.

There are two kinds of peace: (1) peace *with* God, which comes by salvation: "Therefore being justified by faith, we have peace with God through our Lord Jesus Christ" (Rom. 5:1); and (2) the peace *of* God, which comes by your surrender to the will of God. Many Christians have peace *with* God but not the peace *of* God.

"Be careful for nothing; but in every thing by prayer and supplication with thanksgiving let your requests be made known unto God,

"And the peace of God, which passeth all understanding, shall keep your hearts and minds through Christ Jesus."—Phil. 4:6,7.

Too many are expecting the peace of God without surrender. You cannot live a selfish, indifferent life and expect to have the peace of God. There must be the surrender of your life to Him.

Most people, especially thinking people, want to be used of God. (I am getting wise to the people of this generation. Some do not think!) Thinking people want to feel that God has a need for them, a work for them.

People want their earthly needs supplied until Jesus calls them Home. They want to be free of worry, free of fretting about material things.

God gives it—the tither's way.

"Bring ye all the tithes into the storehouse, that there may be meat in mine house, and prove me now herewith, saith the LORD of hosts, if I will not open you the windows of heaven, and pour you out a blessing, that there shall not be room enough to receive it."—Mal. 3:10.

There is His promise to supply. And I have never known God's way to fail.

Paul has the answer in Colossians 3:1–4:

"If ye then be risen with Christ, seek those things which are above, where Christ sitteth on the right hand of God.

"Set your affection on things above, not on things on the earth

"For ye are dead, and your life is hid with Christ in God.

"When Christ, who is our life, shall appear, then shall ye also appear with him in glory."

What are the major thoughts in these four verses? Paul speaks to the Christian:

"Seek those things which are above." "Set your affection on things above." Die to self: "Your life is hid with Christ in God." Christ is coming again, and when He comes we shall be with Him.

Fix your attention on these verses for a few moments.

I. THE AIM OF THE APOSTLE

Colossians was written to establish believers. In the first century there were those who had received Christ as Saviour, but they were not firmly established. Paul was used of God to give inspired words to establish the first-century Christians and also to establish Christians of the twentieth and twenty-first centuries.

Paul wrote the letter to the Romans to establish them in their faith in Christ the Saviour. The great doctrines of grace are expounded.

Paul wrote I Corinthians to the church in Corinth to correct the conduct of the baby Christians. He exposed their sin and shamed them for their disobedience.

Paul wrote Galatians to call the people back to a simple faith in Christ to save. Some teachers had come in with the intention of confusing the Christians by saying that grace is good, but you also must keep the law. Paul declares that we are justified by faith.

"Knowing that a man is not justified by the works of the law, but by the faith of Jesus Christ, even we have believed in Jesus Christ, that we might be justified by the faith of Christ, and not by the works of the law: for by the works of the law shall no flesh be justified."—Gal. 2:16.

The world is the same! The Devil is still working.

Christians still need to be established. So many wax hot, then cold. So many run strong for awhile, then drop by the wayside. Be steadfast!

Paul's aim was to establish the believers: "If ye then be risen with Christ, seek those things which are above."

Let the aim of the apostle be yours. Seek to establish others—your family, your friends. Don't let some failure deter you; keep on trying! Establish yourself! And help to establish others!

II. THE NEED OF BELIEVERS

We are in a constant battle with sin. Paul wrote to Timothy:

"But thou, O man of God, flee these things; and follow after righteousness, godliness, faith, love, patience, meekness.

"Fight the good fight of faith, lay hold on eternal life, whereunto thou art also called, and has professed a good profession before many witnesses."—I Tim. 6:11, 12.

Paul exhorted the Corinthians:

"Therefore, my beloved brethren, be ye stedfast, unmoveable, always abounding in the work of the Lord, forasmuch as ye know that your labour is not in vain in the Lord."—I Cor. 15:58.

1. Some Christians are divisive. See Romans 16:17: "Now I beseech you, brethren, mark them which cause divisions and offenses contrary to the doctrine which ye have learned; and avoid them."

Many churches are plagued with divisive Christians. Often when I come to a church for special services, the pastor will warn me that certain men or families will try to pull me aside and criticize the church and pastor. God spare us from such people! Usually they leave and cause trouble in another church.

2. Some Christians are worldly. That was the fault of Demas. The Bible says, "Demas hath forsaken me, having loved this present world" (II Tim. 4:10).

A worldly Christian is defeated, so he cannot be greatly used, nor can he be filled with the Holy Spirit.

3. Some Christians are "babyish." Paul called the Corinthians "babes in Christ" because they were carnally minded. This prompted envy and strife.

Your greatest need? Lay it out before our God!

I have read the stories of F. B. Meyer, C. I. Scofield, D. L. Moody and George Mueller. Each faced his need. Self was conquered, and Christ was seen.

III. THE SOLUTION

"For ye are dead, and your life is hid with Christ in God" (Col. 3:3). It is by death to self that your life is hid with Christ in God. Dying to self makes real the hidden life. It has been said, "The Christian life is the hidden life."

The hidden life is the safe life. We are hidden in Christ for salvation, like Noah and his family were hidden in the ark.

The hidden life is the justified life. We are hidden in Christ for justification.

The hidden life is the joyful life. Paul could tell us to "rejoice in the Lord" from a prison cell. Many great Christians rejoice when sufferings and privations touch their bodies and lives.

The hidden life is the comfortable life. We are hidden in the warm shelter of His love.

The hidden life is the fruitful life. Jesus said, "Except a corn of wheat fall into the ground and die, it abideth alone: but if it die, it bringeth forth much fruit" (John 12:24).

The hidden life is the invisible life.

"I am crucified with Christ: nevertheless I live; yet not I, but Christ liveth in me: and the life which I now live in the flesh I live by the faith of the Son of God, who loved me, and gave himself for me."—Gal. 2:20.

We are hidden in Christ. The power of God can be ours when we are hidden in Him. SELF will defeat us. When we remain little in our own eyes, we are kept out of the sight of men.

Here is a solemn fact: "Ye are dead"—dead to criticism and dead to praise.

Here is a secure fact: "Your life is hid with Christ in God." Your position is secure! Nothing can take you out of His hand.

Here is a satisfying fact: "When Christ, who is our life,

shall appear, then shall ye also appear with him in glory" (Col. 3:4). He will keep His promise. Christ is coming, and we shall be caught up with Him.

Here is a searching fact: Unless we die we bear no fruit. I repeat: "Except a corn of wheat fall into the ground and die, it abideth alone: but if it die, it bringeth forth much fruit" (John 12:24).

The fruit of the Spirit is "love, joy, peace, longsuffering, gentleness, goodness, faith, Meekness, temperance" (Gal. 5:22, 23). The fruit of the Christian life is another Christian. We are to point others to Christ! Are we doing it?

HOW CAN I BE AN EFFECTIVE CHRISTIAN?

In this message I want to answer your questions: "How can I serve God? How can I be the best pastor I can possibly be, the best Sunday school teacher, the best missionary? What can I do? What does it take? What are some of the qualities, some of the characteristics of one who is serving God and doing what ought to be done?"

When I spoke on failure I mentioned the sixty thousand people or so who commit suicide in one year. Doubtless, the great majority knew nothing of Christ. Many Christians do not have victory and are not doing the job God wants them to do.

I share with you some things that will help us be strong in the Lord.

A man in his late thirties, who had been preaching some nineteen years, came to me and announced, "I'm through. I'm quitting. I'm not going to preach another sermon." Boy, he was tough!

"Wait a minute!" I said. "Are you saved?"

"Yes sir."

"Have you been called to preach?"

"Yes sir."

"Then you can do nothing but preach. You have no other choice."

He said, "Yes, I have. I've been criticized. I have fought opposition everywhere I've gone. It seems nobody wants to follow. I'm tired, so I'm giving it up."

And he did give it up, in spite of everything I could say. He quit the ministry and has turned to another business.

How can we be our best for our Lord? Let me share a few things with you:

I. FAITH

Jesus said, "Have faith in God" (Mark 11:22). "So then faith cometh by hearing, and hearing by the word of God" (Rom. 10:17). Faith is our great need. We have to believe and know that God is real, that He is with us.

You ask, "How can I build my faith?"

1. By the Word of God. Read this Book and let it speak to you. Hebrews, chapter 11, and a number of other places deal with faith. Begin from the beginning and go all the way through. See the faith of Abraham, Moses, Joshua, Gideon—the whole crowd—and build your life on faith as pictured in the holy Word of God.

2. Build your faith on past experiences. Has God ever failed you? No, and He never will. When you will put your faith and trust in Him, He will see you through. Build your faith on your personal experiences.

Too bad that some go ahead and do something for God, then two weeks later come back complaining, "God failed me." No, He never has and never will.

3. Build your faith on what happened to others. If God did something for another, He will do it for you, since He is no respecter of persons. If He blessed Spurgeon, Moody, Torrey, Billy Sunday, Finney and others, He will bless you.

We make a mistake. We build up the name of George Mueller—I have over and over again used him as a great man of prayer—but I have the same promises that George Mueller had! So do you!

We build up Spurgeon. Oh, I love the name of Spurgeon! I have read his sermons most all my life. I love to read them. Spurgeon! Just magnificent! I have been to the Spurgeon Tabernacle in London on two occasions. I spoke there briefly one Wednesday evening in a prayer meeting. But what God has done for Spurgeon and others, He will do for you. Believe this.

Build your faith on the Word of God and upon your own personal experiences, then upon the experiences of others who have been greatly used of God.

II. CONVICTIONS

For God to use your life, there must be rock-ribbed, unchanging convictions now, tomorrow and for the rest of your life.

We live in a strange day. The men I preached for last year and trusted, may change before I go back again. Some have. They may change in the way they part their hair—and how much they have! Now they have a beard, whereas they did not before. I mean, we see changes all around. Am I right? The family style of living changes. People change.

Get convictions on what is right and wrong, then hold to them. Don't vary, don't change. Hold strong to your convictions.

Have conviction about the Word of God, and let no one change you. This is God's holy, inspired, infallible Word. Do not argue; just stand up and preach it.

Have conviction on salvation, on the local church, on baptism.

Some confusing things are going on today, even in Baptist

churches. I saw one the other day that said one must come forward and stay in the church a whole year before the pastor would baptize him.

I handed the preacher my Bible and said, "Show me that in the Bible."

He backed up and said, "Well, it's not in there, but we think it's a good plan. Why baptize a man who's not going to be faithful?"

I said, "You can't tell about that, so you are to do what the Book says."

At Pentecost they didn't have Sunday school literature or church manuals to go by, but they baptized three thousand people. The book of Acts says the Philippian jailor and his family were baptized at once. Get your convictions from the Bible and stand by them.

We ask those who take a position in our church—some 350 Sunday school teachers, 95 deacons, 115 ushers—to agree to this pledge:

(1) Do you know you are saved?

(2) Will you live a separated Christian life?

(3) Will you be faithful to the stated services of the church—Sunday morning, Sunday night and Wednesday night?

(We elect no one who would not promise to attend all three services. I use my motto "Three to Thrive.")

(4) Will you be loyal to the church and the pastor and the program of the church?

That pledge is necessary. Some people delight in being disloyal. When they get a little revolutionary idea, they want to fight the preacher, the church and keep everything from going forward. Usually there is one or two in every church. So ask for loyalty.

Salvation, separation, faithfulness, loyalty! We try to build in our people some convictions about right and wrong.

III. VISION

Without vision the people perish. In all our work, vision is a must. Some people may start out with a vision of doing something great for God, then lose that vision. Little discouragements come along, handicaps and opposition face them, so they lose the vision of winning souls and building a Sunday school.

Get a vision before you and keep it there. Trust God, have faith in Him and keep moving along. You must get a vision.

It doesn't bother me one bit when a young person walks in and says, "Brother Roberson, God has called me to be an evangelist. I want to hold good meetings and do a big job for God." Big things. He may be twenty or twenty-one, but he will say, "When I get out of here, I want to accomplish something big for God."

I encourage him! I don't say, "Now, son, take it easy. Don't be in a hurry. Don't get stirred up too much." Rather I say, "Go ahead and do it!"

I need not tell him he will face opposition. My job is to encourage him to think big for God, do great things for God.

A young man walked in my office one day some years ago and said, "My name is _____ _____. I'm going to check your church and see what you are doing and write it down." He stayed around a number of days, and he took a book full of notes.

We had a big prayer meeting on Wednesday night. A large choir was there to sing. All the ushers were present. The orchestra played. It was a tremendous service. He took notes on everything. In Sunday school he went to every meeting and to visitation. He took it all down.

Then he walked in to me and said, "I think I've got it. I know what I want to do now."

He left us and went up to Rhode Island, the worst state in the Union for building a church, for Rhode Island is mostly Roman Catholic. He found an empty church building between two villages nine miles apart! He rented that empty church building and began to work. Before his death in his early forties, he was averaging fourteen hundred in Sunday school. And that from nothing! He began with just his faith in God and the Word of God. And after having been with us for just a short time and taking some notes of what he wanted to do, he got a vision. He said, "If you can do it here, I know I can do it up there." And he did.

Get your vision and ask God to help you, to use you.

I wish I could tell you all the things that race through my mind. I can see the little fellow walking down the aisle of our empty church during the week and saying to me, "I'm So-and-so"—and he gave his name. "I just got saved the other day."

"Where were you?" I asked.

"In Buffalo, New York."

"Who led you to the Lord?"

"Hyman Appelman was in the city, and when I saw that tent and his name up there, I wanted to hear him. I sat in the back, and the Lord convicted me that I was a lost sinner. I walked up front and said, 'I want to be saved,' and Hyman Appelman led me to the Lord. Then I said, 'Now, Dr. Appelman, what should I do next? I know I am saved now.'

"Dr. Appelman told me, 'Go to Chattanooga and see Lee Roberson.' So here I am. What do I do?"

Not knowing a thing about him, I said, "Well, son, do you know you're saved?"

"I do know I've been born again."

He joined our church, and I baptized him. He stayed around for many months. I gave him a Bible to read, gave him books and got him a place to stay, all because of Hyman's friendship.

After a short time he came to me and said, "I don't feel

called to be a preacher nor a missionary, but I do feel called to be a Christian businessman."

He left us, went to Philadelphia, rented an old house, went down in the basement, put in some tables and began his business. From that beginning in a rented basement of an old house in Philadelphia, he became a multimillionaire. He died in his fifties, but I had the joy of seeing what he could do.

His money is still being used today. Tennessee Temple has received quite a few million dollars. He got a vision and said, "I can do it!" And from nothing, God took him and used him mightily.

Preachers and preacher boys, don't let anybody tell you that you can't do it. You can, with God's help. "If God be for us, who can be against us?" (Rom. 8:31). Let God help you do it.

Get a vision and hold to that vision.

I prayed about the matter of retiring from Highland Park Baptist Church, though I do not like that word *retirement.* After many months God led me to retire at seventy-three plus. I thought God might use me in some other field.

As soon as I retired from the church, invitations started coming from all over the nation. A church has me for one or two days. I have been following that plan now for years. That seemed to be what God wanted me to do.

I still keep my interest in the church, and I am still the chancellor of Tennessee Temple University. I have my office there and a secretary. But God has blessed and used this new ministry in a very unique way.

Get the vision of what you can do, then let God open up doors. He will show you the next step.

I will stop on that point, but I could give you much more on having a vision.

IV. ENDURANCE

Paul said, "Thou therefore endure hardness, as a good soldier of Jesus Christ" (II Tim. 2:3). Nothing is accomplished without steadfastness. Nothing is achieved without enduring and continuing on in spite of all circumstances.

Enduring means you have to die to self.

Years ago I used to sit and talk often with Dr. George W. Truett, a Southern Baptist. I have heard him say, "Sometimes I go home on Sunday night so discouraged that I tell my wife, 'I'm resigning.' But Monday morning I get up and 're-sign' and go again." He kept on going for forty-five years. (George Truett was a postmillennialist when he was among us, but he is "pre-" now!)

I knew J. Frank Norris well. I talked to him in Detroit over two hours one night. What a man! I can recall times in his life when he was tempted to be discouraged. But he was a fighter! And those times of discouragement are true of all.

But we have to endure. We have to die to self. We must be filled with the Spirit.

Be determined. "This one thing I do" (Phil. 3:13).

V. SUBMISSION

"Father,...not my will, but thine, be done" (Luke 22:42), the Lord Jesus said. Be submissive to your blessed Lord and follow the great example of the Son of God who prayed, "Thy will be done." Know His will, then do His will. Be submissive.

Neither husband nor wife should rebel here. Sometimes one or the other gets a little tired and feels like there is too much, too big a cost. But be submissive to the Lord, no matter what it takes, and God will see you through.

Evaluate things around you. See them as they are; then pray the Lord to direct you, to show you His will; then follow it.

Sometimes you get out of harness; sometimes you get on

the sideline, fold your hands and say, "I don't think I can do it. I'm a failure. I can't do it." But put your faith in God and read the Word again. Read the Psalms, where David had his struggles. Read on, then rest in the Lord, wait on the Lord, and have faith in God.

Read Psalm 37:3,4. Just keep on reading and trusting and having faith. Keep submitting to the Lord! Tell Him you are in His hands. Ask Him to guide you, to direct you, to show you His will. Be submissive.

I picked up a book the other day which has been out of print a long time. It told the story of the late Henry Grady, once editor of *The Atlanta Constitution*. There are two worldwide papers in Atlanta, *The Atlanta Constitution* and *The Atlanta Journal*.

As a young man, Henry Grady became noted as an orator. Oh, how this famous man could speak! Incidentally, he died at age thirty-nine.

I read the story about his going to a YMCA meeting back when it meant Young Men's Christian Association. (It does not quite mean that now.) This great citywide meeting was in Atlanta, in a big auditorium. Crowds came.

The last night of that Young Men's Christian Association meeting, all the speakers were on the platform. Henry Grady was standing down front, this editor of *The Atlanta Constitution* and famous orator. At the closing, all the leaders of the YMCA were called to the platform. They joined hands and were about to sing, "Blest be the tie that binds our hearts in Christian love," when one of the men said, "Just a moment. Mr. Grady, come and join hands with us as we sing."

Mr. Grady shook his head no. He folded his arms and put his head down as they sang the song. When they finished, he got up and walked out.

The next morning Henry Grady called all the YMCA leaders into his office and said:

Gentlemen, I apologize for last night. I am sorry for what I did, but I couldn't help it. Gentlemen, my mother led me to the Lord years ago. I am a child of God. I believe in what you are doing, but I am not now in fellowship with God. I have been so busy making money and running a paper and traveling all over the country that I have lost my contact with God. I have stopped going to church, stopped reading my Bible. Yes, I am a Christian but out of fellowship with God.

They prayed with him, then left. Henry Grady walked through the offices of *The Atlanta Constitution* and told his men, "I'm leaving. I'll not tell you where I'm going nor when I'll be back."

He left. With his suitcase in hand, he caught the train back to Rome, Georgia, sixty miles below Chattanooga.

He got off the train in Rome and walked through town to his old home. His mother was still living there, but his father was gone.

He knocked on the door. His mother came to the door. She was so happy to see him! She had not seen him much. He had been too busy running a paper and speaking over the whole country.

When he got inside, he said, "Mama, I want you to treat me just like you did when I was a little boy, back when I first got saved. I want you to pray at the table. I want you to read the Bible. At night when I go to bed, I want you to tuck me in. Then I want you to kneel down beside my bed and pray the same way you did when I was a boy."

His mother said, "Well, Son, I'll do whatever you say."

The great Henry Grady stayed there. Day after day she read the Word of God to him. They sat and talked about the Bible, about holy things, about what he should be and what he should do. At the table they would read and pray. At night she read and prayed by the side of his bed, tucked him in and bade him good-night.

After two weeks had gone by, he walked in and said to his mother, "Mama, it's settled. I'm back where I used to be. I'm right with God. I want God to have His way in my life. I'm surrendered to Him. Everything's all right, Mama. Thank you, Mama."

They had prayer together, and he left for Atlanta.

They say that the latter days of Henry Grady were his greatest. He gave one single address that became famous worldwide, both in the North and the South. The North and the South were having some problems, as you know, between 1850 and 1889; and he was the speaker who was used so mightily in a Christian way to stir the hearts of many.

Sometimes we have to get back. Have you lost something along the way? Do you remember the old days—the days when you first began your ministry—how you prayed and trusted God? Get back to the same thing, just like you felt then.

There was a day when you wept, then you got away from weeping. Ask God to help you get back to that. Let there be a submission beyond anything you have ever known. Sell out to God.

The final word is

VI. COMPASSION

Faith, conviction, vision, endurance, submission, compassion. We have to care! "But when he saw the multitudes, he was moved with compassion on them, because they fainted, and were scattered abroad, as sheep having no shepherd" (Matt. 9:36).

We have lost our compassion, have we not? We don't care like we used to. There are not many tears shed in churches over sinners now.

A fellow walked down Market Street in Chattanooga, left the sidewalk and walked into the parking lot to get in his car. As he did so, two men jumped him and beat him to the ground. He screamed for help. They beat him more, kicked his body, bruised his face, then robbed him of every penny he had.

Lying on the ground, he called for help. Hundreds walked by on the sidewalk on the busiest street in our city, but not a one came to his rescue.

I went to see him in the hospital. I asked, "Sir, what in the world happened to you?" He told me; then he said, "Brother Roberson, what has happened to people? I shouted for help, but not a one came."

That is also true in our churches. We just don't care much anymore. We are not much concerned about others anymore. Let's get back to the compassion that reaches out after people, that searches them out, that gets them to Christ.

O God, help us to care!

I was preaching in Topeka, Kansas. A man drove me into Kansas City to get a plane about three o'clock in the morning. At the airport I was sitting in a chair. A man came and sat down beside me, opened up the morning newspaper and began reading it. I was tired, weary and sleepy, so I paid little attention to what he was doing.

As soon as he had finished reading, he threw the paper down on the chair beside me and walked away. He had folded that paper in a way that it was apparent he had been reading a certain article. I picked it up and began to read it.

It told the story of a mother in Kansas City who was teaching her son, five years old, how to make his ABCs. The little fellow would take the pencil and try to imitate his mother. He did that a few times but didn't do it right. Everything was backwards. He could not make the letters come out right. She scolded him, and he tried again.

The father came walking in. Looking down and seeing what was happening, he said, "Mother, let me show him how."

She got up. He sat down, took the pencil and began making the ABCs. He said, "Now, Son, you make them like Daddy, in just the same way."

The boy tried.

The father said, "No, Son, you're not doing it right. Here, watch me carefully. Here is how you make A and B and C and D."

The boy tried and failed again.

This time the father got out of his chair, reached down, took the boy by the arms, raised him up in the air, crushed his arms in his big hands, threw the boy's body on the floor and trampled on him with his feet, fracturing his skull and breaking a lot of bones.

The newspaper said (it had happened just a few hours before), "The boy is in the hospital unconscious and at the point of death. The father is behind bars in the county jail."

When I read that story, I got so mad! I love kids. I began Camp Joy for children in 1946. We take three thousand a year free. Yes, I love children. I picked up that newspaper and began walking up and down the airport, holding that paper in my hand. I thought, *Man! If I could get hold of a rascal like that, I would beat him to a pulp!* Imagine a man trampling on his own son, five years old, and breaking his little body, fracturing his skull and putting him in the hospital, unconscious! What in the world is wrong with the man!

All of a sudden God seemed to stop me in the middle of that almost empty airport at three o'clock in the morning. I seemed to hear Him say, "You're upset about a mother and a father and a little son whom you've never seen. But down the street from your church on Bailey Avenue there are people lost and going to Hell whom you have never been to see one time. You have never shed a tear over them. You have never been excited about them."

I was excited about that situation and about that family in Kansas City, but right near me were people eternally lost whom I had neglected and failed to reach.

Maybe that is the same with you. You can get excited about Germany, about Russia, about Israel, about Tripoli, about Granada. You can get excited about the Philippines, but do you ever get excited about the folks who live right down the street who need Christ?

THE ANSWER IS LOVE— LOVE FOR YOUR ENEMIES

"Ye have heard that it hath been said, Thou shalt love thy neighbour, and hate thine enemy.

"But I say unto you, Love your enemies, bless them that curse you, do good to them that hate you, and pray for them which despitefully use you, and persecute you;

"That ye may be the children of your Father which is in heaven: for he maketh his sun to rise on the evil and on the good, and sendeth rain on the just and on the unjust.

"For if ye love them which love you, what reward have ye? do not even the publicans the same?

"And if ye salute your brethren only, what do ye more than others? do not even the publicans so?

"Be ye therefore perfect, even as your Father which is in heaven is perfect."—Matt. 5:43–48.

"But love ye your enemies, and do good, and lend, hoping for nothing again; and your reward shall be great, and ye shall be the children of the Highest: for he is kind unto the unthankful and to the evil."—Luke 6:35.

The Christian must not sidestep any issue. With courage, face every question. Don't foolishly imagine you can live righteously without enemies. Any stand for Christ will bring opposition. Paul said, "Yea, and all that will live godly in Christ Jesus shall suffer persecution" (II Tim. 3:12).

Christ had enemies. Throughout His ministry, people hounded Him, criticized Him and sought to destroy Him. Finally, when they crucified Him, they then imagined that they had brought Him to His end.

The Apostle Paul had enemies. He who had turned his back on fame and fortune; he who had turned from the easy road to take the hazardous path; he who had left the selfish, sinful way for the way of the cross, had enemies. And because of enemies, he suffered much. He was beaten cruelly. Paul tells us, "Of the Jews five times received I forty stripes save one." His life was often imperiled because of "false brethren." Enemies succeeded in bringing him to his death.

The Apostle Peter had enemies. They fought against him, belittled him, derided him. But did Peter falter? Never. Notice his words given in I Peter 4:12–16:

"Beloved, think it not strange concerning the fiery trial which is to try you, as though some strange thing happened unto you:

"But rejoice, inasmuch as ye are partakers of Christ's sufferings; that, when his glory shall be revealed, ye may be glad also with exceeding joy.

"If ye be reproached for the name of Christ, happy are ye; for the spirit of glory and of God resteth upon you: on their part he is evil spoken of, but on your part he is glorified.

"But let none of you suffer as a murderer, or as a thief, or as an evildoer, or as a busybody in other men's matters.

"Yet if any man suffer as a Christian, let him not be ashamed; but let him glorify God on this behalf."

With these illustrations, we consider what the Bible commands us to do.

I. WE ARE TO LOVE OUR ENEMIES

"But I say unto you, Love your enemies, bless them that curse you, do good to them that hate you, and pray for them which despitefully use you, and persecute you."—Matt. 5:44.

Love is the message of the Bible. The world is selfish, mean and vindictive; but God's message is love.

First, love is essential for Christlikeness. No one can be like the Master unless he loves his enemies. It is easy to love those who love us, but we are commanded to love those who hate us and despise us.

Christ is love, and throughout His life upon the earth we see the manifestation of His love. He loved those who spoke against Him. He loved those who drove the nails in His hands and feet. He loved those who cursed Him and reviled Him. Now, if we are to be like Him, we too must love.

Second, love is essential to growth in grace. You may gain in position and prominence, but you cannot grow in grace without the love of God in your heart. Hate defeats growth. The motivating power to growth in grace is love. Hatred stunts and starves. Love grows and develops.

In a world built on the principles of hatred, could it be that this is the reason why many Christians do not grow in grace? They follow the world; hence, they are brought into the realm of hatred.

Third, love is essential to Christian work. Soul winning is the main work, and this cannot be done without love. It is love that helps us see the need of the worst of men. It is love that leads us to look beyond certain evil and disagreeable personalities and see the need of eternal souls.

In this regard, I must simply ask you to see the Lord Jesus. He loved the poorest and the most despicable, the beggars and the outcasts, the souls of the dishonest men like Zacchaeus and the thief on the cross; yea, He loved them all.

We will only be at our best when we have love for others. If we have animosity in our hearts, we cannot do the work Christ has called us to do.

The Word commands us to love our enemies, to bless them that curse us.

II. WE ARE TO DO GOOD TO THEM THAT HATE US

The plain teaching of our Master is to love the ones who hate us and seek their best interests.

The Apostle Paul gives us a word on doing good to those who hate us: "Therefore if thine enemy hunger, feed him; if he thirst, give him drink: for in so doing thou shalt heap coals of fire on his head" (Rom. 12:20).

These are strange and interesting words. We are to feed our enemies who are hungry and give them drink if they thirst. By so doing, we heap coals of fire on their heads.

In this day, modernism is rampant throughout the country. Modernism tells you to find the good in every man, or it tells you to rationalize, that we all have weaknesses. But Paul says we are to love our enemies, to feed them, to give them drink.

Jesus said, 'Do good to them that hate you. Speak kindly of those who speak against you. Don't return evil for evil. When unkind words are spoken, return with kind words.'

We are to do acts of kindness, says Paul here in Romans. Instead of the old "eye for an eye, tooth for a tooth" philosophy, we are to return good for evil.

May I insert here that it is important to do the right thing. We must not defer, delay and procrastinate. The good that may be resident within our hearts must be expressed now.

Joseph and Nicodemus loved Jesus, but they waited until He was dead to express their love. As they carried His body to the grave, I am sure they had some pangs of regret. What they did for Jesus was wonderful, but they had failed to stand by Him while He was living.

Do what God would have you do now. Christ is our supreme example in this regard. He came to earth to die for sinners. He manifested love and graciousness of spirit toward all men. Some turned to Him; many turned against Him; but toward all, Christ was ever the same.

The answer is love. So we must do good to them that hate us.

III. WE ARE TO PRAY FOR OUR ENEMIES

"And pray for them which despitefully use you, and persecute you."—Matt. 5:44.

The victory is won when you can truly pray for your enemies. In this again we are given a divine example when Christ on the cross prayed for His enemies: "Father, forgive them; for they know not what they do." If He prayed for others, then we too must pray for others.

Let us notice some things about praying for our enemies:

First, prayer changes bitterness to sweetness. I have known men whose lives were centered around bitterness. They could not pray. But when they turned to loving their enemies, prayer became vital and real, bitterness vanished, and there was a sweetness of soul.

Second, prayer moves the hearts of our enemies. Perhaps we can say little to those who are opposed to us, but we can certainly pray for them. If your enemies are unsaved, then pray for their salvation. If your enemies are Christians, then pray that they will grow in grace. Remember this: for your prayer to be effective, it must be in the Spirit of the Lord Jesus Christ.

Third, pray with one eye on Jesus and the other on sinners. In loving your enemies and praying for them, no one can help you like the Saviour, our inspiration and our

encouragement. He will help you in prayer for your enemies. When sinners see in us a concern and a compassion,
they will be drawn toward Christ.

Now, before you can love your enemies, the following
must take place:

(1) Know Jesus Christ as your Saviour. When you become
a new creature, you can love others.

*"Therefore if any man be in Christ, he is a new creature: old
things are passed away; behold, all things are become new."*—II
Cor. 5:17.

(2) Be a partaker of the nature of Christ. Hear the apostle as he said to the church in Philippi, "Let this mind be in
you, which was also in Christ Jesus." To be Christlike is
more than the mere recitation of words: be like Him in
action and in deed.

(3) The Holy Spirit must control your life. If you are a
child of God, He lives within; therefore, let Him fully possess and control your life.

(4) Constantly feed on the Word of God. This world will
teach hate and revenge; Christians must be guided by love
and mercy. Therefore, read your Bible and practice the
teaching of this infallible Word.

Let the spirit of forgiveness permeate your life so you can
exercise the forgiving spirit toward others.

In a Highland village lived a shepherd and his little
daughter. He would take her with him when he went out over
the moors to tend and fold the sheep. The daughter loved to
hear her father call the sheep with the shepherd's call,
sounding free and beautiful down the wind over the moors.

By and by the little girl became a beautiful young woman
and went off to the great city. At first her letters came regularly every week. Then intervals between them grew longer.
Finally they ceased altogether.

There were rumors too in the village that the shepherd's

daughter had been seen in wild company and in questionable places. At length, a lad from the village who knew her well saw her one day in the city. When he spoke to her, she pretended that she had never seen him before.

When the shepherd heard this, he gathered a few things together and, clad in his shepherd's smock with a shawl wrapped around his shoulders and his shepherd's staff in his hand, set out for the city to seek and find his lost daughter.

Day after day he sought her on the avenues, in the slums and through the alleys of the city—but in vain. Then he remembered how she loved to hear him give the shepherd's call.

Again he set out on his quest of sorrow and love. Several passersby turned with astonishment to look on the shepherd, in his smock and with his staff, as he went up and down the streets sounding the shepherd's call.

At length, in one of the degraded sections of the city, his daughter, sitting in a room with her companions, suddenly had a look of astonishment on her face. There was no doubt about it—it was her father's voice, the shepherd's call.

Swinging wide the door, she rushed out into the street. There her father took her in his arms and carried her with him back to the Highland home.

That is a tiny picture of the love of God for poor sinners. But remember, "God is love." Let us walk in His steps.

HAVE FAITH IN GOD

"And Jesus answering saith unto them, Have faith in God."—
Mark 11.22.

I am eighty-nine years of age. I have been preaching for seventy-one years. I preached my first sermon at age eighteen and was ordained at age twenty.

An interesting story is told about a man in Memphis, Tennessee who got married. He told people everywhere about his happiness. He would add, "If anything were to happen to my wife, I couldn't live."

But one day she did get sick and die, and it almost killed him.

He left Memphis and came to Chattanooga. He was mournful, sad and in a pitiful condition. He went up on beautiful Lookout Mountain to live. There he met a young lady. Before long he fell in love with her. In a short while he asked her to marry him. Then he thought about what he had put on the grave of his wife when she died: THE LIGHT OF MY LIFE HAS GONE OUT.

He married this woman, and they went back to Memphis. After a few months he took her to see the grave of his first wife. But he thought, *I need to change that tombstone.* And he did. When they reached the grave, she read,

THE LIGHT OF MY LIFE HAS GONE OUT,
BUT I STRUCK ANOTHER MATCH.

I am striking another match tonight! I want to keep on going for the Lord.

The foundation for my message is,

"And Jesus answering saith unto them, Have faith in God."—Mark 11:22.

"And the apostles said unto the Lord, Increase our faith."—Luke 17:5.

"So then faith cometh by hearing, and hearing by the word of God."—Rom. 10:17.

"Now faith is the substance of things hoped for, the evidence of things not seen."—Heb. 11:1.

In a recent meeting an audience asked me, "What is the one thing that has kept you going for over seventy years?" Without a moment's hesitation, I answered, "Faith in God."

If I keep my eyes on the Lord, I can keep going. If I keep His promises in my mind, His presence with me, His power upon me by the Holy Spirit, I can rest in Him.

Being faithful can give you added strength for any burden. When faithful to the Lord, the blessings of God will be upon you, and He will give you courage.

The pastor, the missionary, the teacher, the average Christian—all need great faith. The Master Teacher, the great Son of God, the crucified Saviour, the risen One, the One who is coming again, commanded, "Have faith in God."

I. FAITH IN GOD ALWAYS WINS

Faith is a winning attitude. Faith is positive; doubt is negative. In this evil world, faith is the one thing that is necessary. With faith in God, we are on the winning side. We can say with the Apostle Paul, "For I know whom I have believed, and am persuaded that he is able to keep that which I have committed unto him against that day" (II Tim. 1:12).

Faith in Christ makes you a child of God. Do you know

Him today? I don't mean just church membership or baptism, but have you actually met the Lord Jesus? When you are saved, you are in God's family and can pray, "Our Father which art in heaven."

God allowed me to be pastor of one church for forty years and six months. I baptized sixty-three thousand people, then retired and began to travel and preach in other churches. I have been in over eighteen hundred different churches in all parts of the nation and in some foreign countries. I find this: they minimize salvation.

A little boy about eight, ten or twelve comes forward and gets saved. He just stands there. People seem unconcerned about him and rather push him aside. Yet that is the greatest thing that will ever happen to him.

Lay hold on everything God offers you. "If ye shall ask any thing in my name, I will do it," God promised. There are thirty-two thousand promises in the Bible. A Christian can walk the life of faith in God, believe Him and trust Him. Don't be a loser! Be a winner!

I went to see a dear eighty-year-old man down on McCallie Avenue in Chattanooga. He was living alone. He was rather infirm and not very strong. When I asked him, "Are you saved?" he answered, "I don't believe in that at all. I'll have no part in any of that." I told him that without Christ, he was lost for all eternity, condemned and going to Hell. He said, "Well, that doesn't bother me at all."

I went on and witnessed to him. Then when I was through, he said, "Christians are funny people. I have just as many friends as any of you. I don't need Christ. I don't need anything or anyone. I have everything I want." He laughed as I left.

But in a few days this eighty-year-old man died. I went to his funeral. There I noticed something: Counting the minister, there were eight people present. He had boasted about having so many friends, but where were they?

Life is lonely, pitiful and miserable without Christ. Faith in the Lord changes everything and makes us winners.

II. FAITH IN GOD GIVES PEACE

Abraham, Joseph, Moses, David, Paul, John and others had their troubles in life, but they had peace of heart. Jesus said:

"Peace I leave with you, my peace I give unto you: not as the world giveth, give I unto you. Let not your heart be troubled, neither let it be afraid."—John 14:27.

We can have peace in times of affliction, when the body may be weak. Paul had a thorn in the flesh, but he had faith in God. We see tragedy all around us, but faith in God will bring one through, no matter what the sorrow may be.

Our church sent a young lady, Frances Wood, out to Africa as a missionary. There she met and married a young man, Michael Warburton, an engineer. They had a little home on the mission compound. He did his engineering work while she did her mission work. They were very happy. We sent them an offering each month from the church.

One morning she went out to get breakfast at the little grass-covered hut where they lived. When it was ready, she said, "Mike, come to eat." There was no response. She called again. Still no response. She went back to the bed where he was lying.

He said, "Honey, I can't move." He was paralyzed from his waist down and couldn't move the muscles in his legs.

He was taken to the hospital. The doctors sent him on to London, England, saying they couldn't do anything for him.

Michael Warburton said during this time, "I want to be a missionary. I'm going back to the field with my wife, and we will serve God as missionaries." Right now he is doing that very thing. Still paralyzed and in a motorized wheelchair, he preaches with great power.

I went to college wearing a homemade shirt, made by my mother out of a flour sack. I didn't have a nickel to my name. I walked and hitchhiked for 150 miles. When I got to school, I went into the dean's office and told him I would have to work to get through school because I had no money. He said, "I'll give you a job." The job was washing dishes in the dining hall. I was willing to do anything.

I began that job on that very first day. I washed dishes. The twenty-five cents an hour I got was applied to my school bill.

I had faith while in my poverty. I believed God. I believed He had called me and that I had to serve Him.

There is faith in the hour of death. Often I have seen this faith when people come to the end of life. Dr. Charles Weigle, who wrote "No One Ever Cared for Me Like Jesus," lived on the campus of Tennessee Temple for the last fifteen years of his life. He was a magnificent man, a great songwriter and a man of great faith. Up to the age of ninety-five, that faith in God was evident in his life, and it controlled his life.

We had a big Sunday evening service in the downtown Memorial Auditorium. Every seat was filled. Dr. Weigle was there. It was his ninety-fifth birthday. A big three-hundred-voice choir used some of his songs. He had written hundreds of them. It was a beautiful hour. Many people were saved that night.

As I took him back to his room in the old music building, he said, "I had a great time. I have seen nothing like this before. It is not bad to be ninety-five; it's a picnic! This is the best thing that ever happened to me. Praise God! This is wonderful!"

I said, "I just wanted you to know how much we love you and want to do what we can to help you."

Dr. Weigle had faith when his hour of death came. We too must have this faith.

III. FAITH IN GOD GIVES INSPIRATION

Faith awakens my heart and inspires me to go on. David said in Psalm 23, "The LORD is my shepherd; I shall not want." Paul said in Romans 8, "And we know that all things work together for good to them that love God, to them who are the called according to his purpose."

Faith in God gives inspiration. You cannot read nor recite these verses without a surge of encouragement.

Some hours are dark or sad. We all have them. Faith in God inspires us. When our body is weak or in the hour of temptation or when all men forsake us, we look to God for inspiration and help.

Paul said, "But none of these things move me, neither count I my life dear unto myself, so that I might finish my course with joy" (Acts 20:24). Paul had a Gibraltar faith. He was a determined man, a confident man, a courageous man. Nothing could move him from his faith in God. Dangers, enemies, hunger, persecution, prison, suffering, even death, could not shake him.

Men may fail us, but God—never!

IV. FAITH IN GOD MOVES ME TO OBEDIENCE

Samuel said, "Behold, to obey is better than sacrifice, and to hearken than the fat of rams" (I Sam. 15:22). My faith and my love will move me to obedience. It is inconsistent to say we have faith in God, then not listen to Him or obey Him.

We are witnesses for Him: "...ye shall be witnesses unto me" (Acts 1:8). A witness tells what he knows. Then God brings the fruit.

The local church is to be obedient. Jesus said, "If ye love me, keep my commandments." The Great Commission has been given; now we must obey it.

A man came to me complaining about his many troubles. He said he prayed but God didn't answer his prayers. When

I asked him, "Are you saved?" he said he had been saved for nine years.

Next, I asked him where his church membership was. "Oh, I don't belong to a church. And I haven't been baptized. And I don't care to." I told him he couldn't disobey the Lord and expect answers to his prayers.

Faith moves us to obedience.

V. FAITH IN GOD CAN CHANGE ANY SITUATION

Moses and Israel stood between the armies of Egypt and the Red Sea. It was an impossible situation; yet God opened the Red Sea, and Israel crossed on dry land, but the Egyptians were swallowed up in the water. All things are possible with God.

Elijah stood on Mount Carmel. The rebellious Israelites were on one side, and Elijah and a water-soaked altar were on the other. When God answered prayer, the people cried out, "The LORD, he is the God."

Faith in God can change any situation and give new hope in time of trouble. Faith gives courage, even in the face of death and problems. Faith can give strength and power to a defeated man.

"Have faith in God," commanded the Lord, and that command was meant for every one of us.

A preacher called me and said through tears, "I'm in real trouble. The people here have turned against me. They want me to leave. Please help me." I couldn't do a thing for him but pray. I promised him that God would help him if he had faith.

Sometimes we fail and have to pray, "O God, correct me, and make me be what You want me to be."

My age doesn't relieve me of that necessity. Even today I can say that I still have faith in God.

Faith can change any situation. In Acts 16, there was a revival in the jail. Faith can also change a whole city. Read about Jonah in Nineveh. Faith can change a lions' den into a luxurious bedroom chamber. Read about Daniel in the lions' den. Faith can change a slime pit into an easy chair. Read about Jeremiah. Read Hebrews 11, the great faith chapter. Faith will change your home, your business, your attitude and your church.

Have faith in God!

VI. FAITH IN GOD GIVES COMPASSION

Our God is a God of compassion. Take a long, reverent look at Jesus Christ. You see compassion, whether in Nazareth, in Jerusalem or on Calvary.

From Genesis to Revelation we have one great theme—a God of love. He has compassion. He gave His Son to die for us. What distinguished the men of the Bible whom God used? Was it education, money, culture? No, it was compassion.

Faith in God gives compassion. Take a look at this lost world. What is its chief need? The world is crying, "No man cared for my soul." Many are wondering what is going on, but no one is out to help them. We must knock on their doors and witness to them. We must tell them about Jesus' dying on the cross for them. We must give them a Bible or a New Testament.

An article in *Newsweek* shocked me. Advertising for the World Summit for Children, the article said:

> Every two days 2,800 children around the world will die from whooping cough, 8,000 children will die from measles, 4,300 will die from tetanus, 5,500 will die from malaria, 22,000 children will die from diarrhea, and 12,000 children will die from pneumonia.

Think of that! Every two days many children and young people die. And how many of them are saved? I am reminded again that people all around us are dying without Christ and going to an eternal Hell.

The Selfishness of Saints. Maybe they are lost because of our indifference. Missionary work suffers. Don't be an indifferent Christian. Conquer your lukewarmness. Stir yourself up.

The Self-Righteousness of Christians. Many are satisfied just attending the Sunday morning service. And they want it to be fifteen minutes long—no longer. There is no concern for others.

The Sins of Saints. Sin brings weakness as well as forgetfulness to Christians. Beware lest you forget the Lord.

When doubts creep in, have faith in God! When someone tries to plant a seed of unbelief in your heart, have faith in God! When someone says it can't be done, have faith in God! Determine to go on, no matter what the world says. Serve God with faith until He takes you Home!

"Have faith in God." Amen!

THE SPIRIT-FILLED LIFE

"And when he was gone forth into the way, there came one running, and kneeled to him, and asked him, Good Master, what shall I do that I may inherit eternal life?

"And Jesus said unto him, Why callest thou me good? there is none good but one, that is, God.

"Thou knowest the commandments, Do not commit adultery, Do not kill, Do not steal, Do not bear false witness, Defraud not, Honour thy father and mother.

"And he answered and said unto him, Master, all these have I observed from my youth.

"Then Jesus beholding him loved him, and said unto him, One thing thou lackest: go thy way, sell whatsoever thou hast, and give to the poor, and thou shalt have treasure in heaven: and come, take up the cross, and follow me.

"And he was sad at that saying, and went away grieved: for he had great possessions."—Mark 10:17–22.

From this story, think on these simple words, "One thing thou lackest."

What is missing in your life? God may be putting His finger on something that needs to be corrected—something you need to do that you are not doing. "One thing thou lackest." God is speaking to all of us in some way.

Years ago in Louisville, Kentucky, I had a good friend. Of

all the people I've ever met, I think he was the most excep-
tional. He had a terrific memory. He could memorize chapters and whole books of the Bible. This great man and wonderful preacher was ordained in Louisville where I was
also ordained.

I took my first church in Germantown, Tennessee, near
Memphis. He came down and said he wanted to preach,
wanted to be a pastor. I recommended him to a church down
in Mississippi. When he preached for them, they called
him at once! The fellow was fluent and had a beautiful
personality.

He stayed there for about four weeks, then came back to
see me in Memphis to say he didn't like it there. "I'm quitting," he said. When I pointed out that he had been there for
only a month, he said, "I know, but I don't like it. That is not
the place for me. Recommend me to another church."

I went ahead and recommended him to a church in Pine
Bluff, Arkansas. They heard the man speak. They called
him. He stayed three or four weeks, then came back to me
at Memphis, saying he was through with that; would I recommend him to another church?

I said, "No, I've done enough."

He went back to Louisville and died after some years—a
complete failure. He had everything, but he wouldn't stick
to anything. He had a mind, an education, training and personality; but he did not endure, did not keep going.

Do you need to say to God, "O God, something is missing
in my life; help me to correct it, to make it right"?

I know pastors who were good men; they could quote
Scripture and preach wonderful sermons, but they failed
miserably. Something was wrong—maybe something mor-
ally wrong—and they turned aside.

Saul of Tarsus had just about everything a man could ask
for—a brilliant mind, a good education, a high position and

good respect. But he did not know Christ. He was lost.

Thousands of people have something missing in their lives. They need to pray, "O God, make me what You want me to be."

Look at the rich, the influential, the politicians and others. Something is missing, something is wrong, something is not quite hitting right. This may be true of the president or a governor or a senator—it could be true of anyone.

What is missing in YOUR life? Do you *know* that you are born again? Paul said in II Timothy 1:12, "I know whom I have believed." Can you say from your heart, "Yes, Lord, I know I am born again"?

I am not discussing denominationalism, whether you're Baptist or Methodist or Presbyterian. I am asking, Have you received Christ as your personal Saviour? Paul knew whom he had believed.

Peter said in his first epistle, "Unto you therefore which believe he is precious" (2:7). The preciousness of the Lord Jesus Christ is real! Do you know Him?

When I see people fail, I wonder if they are really saved. When I see them come to church for awhile, then quit, I wonder if they are really born again.

The other day one of our big mission boards told me that ten percent of all missionaries they send out come home and never go back. When an average of ten percent turn away after one term on the field, something is wrong.

Check your life. Be set and established in the work of God.

First, do you know that you are saved? Can you say, "Yes! Jesus is mine. I am a child of God"?

I was doing a broadcast one morning in Chattanooga, when a fellow came walking down the aisle. This fine, well-dressed man walked up on the platform, took my hand and said, "Brother Roberson, I've come to tell you that I just got saved!" I rejoiced with him. He continued to tell me that he was driving in from Dalton, Georgia, and while listening to the broadcast, he had gotten saved.

He shook hands with the pianist, the organist and anyone he could find, then came to me again. He told me he lived just south of Chattanooga. I asked what sort of business he was in. He said, "I am pastor of the First Baptist Church, but I was never saved until this morning."

He went home and told his church about it, got baptized and was ordained again.

Church membership is not a sign of the new birth, of knowing Christ as your Saviour. You may be a deacon, a Sunday school teacher, a choir member; but have you been *saved?* If so, can you tell another person how to be saved?

Second, do you have a sense of direction in your life? a calling from God? Do you have a purpose in life? God has a will, a definite purpose, for your life. Will you ask, as did Paul, "What would God have me to do?" then do what He says?

Know God's will for your life and walk with Him every day.

Many people do not have direction for their lives; therefore, they are drifters. The cities are full of them, wandering up and down the streets and living in the alleys and gutters. They have not been born again. They have not been called of God.

I know many are able to say, "Yes, I do have a sense of direction. I know what God wants me to do."

Young man, young woman, Mom, Dad, God has a will for you, a definite spot that He wants you to fill. Will you follow where He leads?

I got to know a young man named Clarence pretty well. One night while Clarence was waiting in his car at a stoplight, a man came up, shot and killed him.

When I heard this story, I went to the funeral home. When I found the room where this young man's body lay, I walked inside. There was only one in the room—a girl. I introduced myself, and we talked for awhile. She had said she didn't know Clarence very well, but I asked her to tell me what she could about him.

She began to recall the incidents of the night. She said when that gunman came up, Clarence was talking to her about being saved. He told her he had been called to preach, but he also said he doubted if he would ever preach. Then she said the gun was shot, killing Clarence. "His last words were, 'I doubt if I will ever preach,'" she said.

What I am trying to emphasize is the necessity of having a sense of direction, knowing God's will for your life.

The world may not agree with you. You may have to change friends and part with some of your family, but go God's way. Serve Him. Obey your Lord.

A young lady, Frances Woods, came down the aisle of our church one Sunday morning, saying that she had been called of God to be a missionary. She was head of the nurses at Campbell's Clinic in Chattanooga, a very fine hospital. "I am called to be a missionary in Africa, and I am going!" Just like that, she told the whole audience.

The next day Dr. Campbell called, asking me to tell Miss Woods she was wrong. She was his employee, and he wanted her on the job. He instructed me to tell the girl to forget that mission work and stay right where she was.

I told him to tell her himself, that I wasn't telling the young lady anything like that. And I didn't.

She has been on the field twenty-five or thirty years. She is a great missionary and serving God well.

Do you have a sense of direction in your life and a desire to know and follow God's will?

Third, do you know the fullness of the Holy Spirit? If you're saved, then you have the Holy Spirit. But does He have you? Are you filled with the Spirit? The Bible tells us in Ephesians 5:18 to "be filled with the Spirit." God wants to fill you.

Have you surrendered your life to Him? The youngest to the oldest Christians need the fullness of the Holy Spirit.

I preached in New Hampshire at a Bible conference on the Holy Spirit. When I had finished I was walking across the grounds. A very dignified man came over and asked me if I were filled with the Holy Spirit. I won't tell you what I answered him.

If you are a child of God, you have Him. But does He have you? Have you given Him full charge? Are you allowing Him to guide and direct in your work and daily activities? That would mean dying to self.

The filling of the Spirit will produce many things:

One is faithfulness. We are told, "Be thou faithful" (Rev. 2:10).

Two, it will give you courage. "Be of good courage" (Ps. 27:14).

Three, you will have a determination. Paul said, "This one thing I do" (Phil. 3:13).

Four, you will bear fruit (Gal. 5:19–26).

Do you have the fullness of the Holy Spirit? Are you controlled by the Holy Spirit? Is He directing your life and working through you?

The world around you is lost, undone, Hell-bound. Lives are changed when you let the Holy Spirit have control. Are you letting Him work through you, Christian? Are you letting the Spirit control your life?

Homes are changed where the Holy Spirit has control. Businesses are changed when the Holy Spirit controls the businesses. Churches are changed when controlled by the Holy Spirit. Great things and mighty things happen when He takes charge. Difficulties and troubles work themselves out when you let the Spirit of God guide you, fill you, empower you.

I was holding a meeting in the state of Florida in a

beautiful church. Only a handful had attended the first two nights.

I was riding down the street with the pastor the third day of the meeting. Suddenly he told me to look to my left, and I would see one of the devils that was killing his church. I looked and saw a man that looked like any other man. The pastor thought he was a devil. And he told me there were three more like him. He had four deacons, and all were devils, he said—just as mean as they could be. They opposed and fought him. They didn't like his ministry and criticized him. He went on and on.

After awhile I discovered the trouble in the meeting was coming from headquarters. The pastor himself had the wrong spirit. I prayed, "O God, help me!" I spoke the next night on being filled with the Spirit. When I gave the invitation, a man came down the aisle and knelt down at the front pew. Other men came down—four in all. I said to myself, *These must be the four deacons.* The four men were crying; so was the audience.

I turned to the pastor, standing behind me holding his Bible, and suggested he join them. He replied, "No sir. They can stay there forever, that bunch of devils! I won't join them."

I thought if they were sincere and coming to make things right, he needed to join with them. But he refused. I then told the pastor he was making a mistake; to let God straighten everything out. Then I walked back to the pulpit.

As the song finished, I watched him walk around, then throw his Bible on the front pew beside these four deacons who had been opposing him, bickering with him. They were on their knees; all of them were crying. The pastor raised his big arm and dropped to his knees. With one arm around two men and the other around the other two, the pastor began to cry out to the Lord: "O God, forgive me! I want to get right with these men and with my church."

They all were praying out loud. The audience quit singing and started crying with them.

After a long time I walked down front and asked the men if they wanted to say something. The preacher asked to speak first, saying he was to blame for it all. "I am the pastor. I have hated these men. We have been disagreeing on everything. We have had trouble. I want to apologize. I want my deacons to forgive me. I want this church to forgive me."

Then the men stood there crying, with their arms around one another.

They shook hands, talked and prayed until almost midnight. God began to move. A church had been dead; nothing was happening; no one was being saved. Then this happened.

When I came back the next night, the crowd had doubled. As I was walking into the service, I put my hand on the door, and someone grabbed my hand. I looked up, and there stood a policeman. He said, "You cannot go in." I thought they were at it again, that they were still fighting and something bad had happened to get the police out there. The police officer said he had orders from headquarters not to allow anyone else in the building because it was overpacked. When I told him I was the preacher, he opened the door and pushed me inside.

I walked into that packed and jammed building. The pastor was standing on the platform, holding his Bible but not saying a word. I walked to the pulpit, preached a brief message and gave an invitation. That night 137 people came forward accepting Christ as Saviour—137! We went on for a few more nights, and every night many were saved!

When the Holy Spirit takes over, something happens.

Fourth, do you have an overwhelming compassion for a lost world? When Jesus saw the multitude, He had compassion on them (Matt. 9:36). Compassion means having the knowledge of man's lost condition. "The soul that sinneth, it shall die" (Ezek. 18:4). The book of Romans says that we have all sinned and come short of the glory of God. All men, all women and all children are lost without Christ.

Again, compassion means having a knowledge of the awfulness of Hell and the glory of Heaven.

Compassion means a knowledge of the simplicity of the Gospel, to win people to the Saviour. Do you have a compassion for a lost and dying world? Are you seeking to point others to our loving Saviour?

That compassion is missing with most people. All fail unless there is that compassion, a desire for souls.

People criticized our bus ministry in Chattanooga. We ran thirty-five buses three times a week. Many were saved as a result. Some members would say it cost too much money. Ah, but one soul is worth it all!

Some will criticize the cost of a revival meeting. Some will say the expense is too great. Oh no! One soul is worth it all!

The simplicity of the Gospel! Knowing Christ as your Saviour!

I preached recently in Baltimore, Maryland. After a good service, I gave an invitation. While standing down front shaking hands with people, a dignified-looking elderly man came by to shake my hand. I felt led to ask him, "Sir, are you a Christian?"

He said he thought so. I asked if he knew for sure. He replied that he didn't, but he thought he might be saved. "I try to be," he said. I told him that he needed Christ, that Christ gives salvation assurance and positive knowledge of a new birth.

I took my Bible and showed him some Scriptures. In a few minutes that fellow was in tears. He put out his hand and said, "Preacher, I have never done this before, but I'm doing it now. I am accepting Jesus Christ as my Saviour."

He was ninety years old! He had retired from a big

government position in Washington, D.C., and was living in Baltimore.

I am afraid that many belong to the church who have never been born again.

Do you have compassion? Do you want to see people saved? Ask God to use you to win them.

Mr. M. J. Parker was in charge of the thirty-five buses at our church. He had gotten saved, and I had baptized him and his wife. Then he asked if he could run one bus and bring in kids. I agreed. He rented an old bus and began running it in a neighborhood. He filled up one, then two, then three, then we began buying them. At one time we owned thirty-five beautiful buses, and he was in charge of all of them.

M. J. Parker was just a humble businessman in the city. I don't know how much money he had, but he gave his whole life to winning people to Christ. He was a sold-out soul winner.

He passed away, and I held the funeral. At the gravesite Mrs. Parker said that when Mr. Parker got saved, he knew God wanted to use him to win people to Christ. He never finished the third grade in school; he could barely read and write. But God used him to win hundreds.

God will use you if you will put your life under His direction.

I held a meeting in Springfield, Tennessee. One little lady was regularly bringing people down the aisle. Miss Abi Burr was a cashier at the First National Bank. She had left the First Baptist Church and gone down to a little mission on the hillside. Every night in my meeting she brought people forward to get saved.

I had been home from the meeting but a few days when I received a phone call saying that Miss Burr was sitting at her desk at work, then in a moment's time she had fallen forward, dead. The family asked if I would have part in the funeral.

I went to the First Baptist Church of Springfield. Many filled the building. I went up to the platform, read the Scripture and prayed.

Then the pastor got up to speak. He said, "Before I give the message, I want the ladies in front to stand. These ladies standing were led to Christ one by one by Miss Abi Burr."

I counted fifty-two ladies. All were led to Christ by this one who had gone from us.

What is missing in your life? salvation? direction? fullness of the Spirit? compassion? or maybe all of them, or maybe none of them?

Do you want God's will done in your life? Will you surrender your all to Him?

GOD'S ABUNDANT BLESSINGS

"For to me to live is Christ, and to die is gain.

"But if I live in the flesh, this is the fruit of my labour: yet what I shall choose I wot not.

"For I am in a strait betwixt two, having a desire to depart, and to be with Christ; which is far better:

"Nevertheless to abide in the flesh is more needful for you.

"And having this confidence, I know that I shall abide and continue with you all for your furtherance and joy of faith;

"That your rejoicing may be more abundant in Jesus Christ for me by my coming to you again."—Phil. 1:21–26.

I have preached in many jails, penitentiaries, prisons and other places of correction since beginning my ministry seventy-one years ago. I have never found a really happy person in any of these places.

Not so, the Apostle Paul. He was in jail in Rome where he wrote the letter to the church in Philippi, yet he was rejoicing in the Lord and telling others to "rejoice in the Lord."

I. THE BLESSING OF A HEALTHY MIND

Paul knew Christ as Saviour. His mind was right; his heart was right. He loved the Lord. He was an educated man, a man of convictions, and in jail because of what he believed. His mind was healthy and free of worry. He rejoiced in the Lord.

Keep your mind healthy, clean and fixed on God. Be alert to the evils of this world through radio, television, magazines, newspapers. Remember: you can have just one thought at a time, and it will be either good or bad. So read the right things. Put good things into your mind.

Many books are sent to me, some good and some bad. Some I discard. Some I read put good things into my mind. Much of television is dangerous. Stay away from that which is dirty.

II. THE BLESSING OF AN ACTIVE MEMORY

Paul could not forget the blessings God had given him. He had a happy heart. He remembered his salvation— recorded in Acts 9:1–6—which happened when he was on his way to Damascus to do harm to believers.

Remember what God has done for you, especially when He saved your soul, and His daily guidance.

Remember how God has answered your prayer. Remember His guidance. Where would we be without the Lord!

I began preaching at age eighteen. At age twenty I became the pastor of a church in Memphis. When I left there, I went to Greenbrier, Tennessee for three years in a little country church. Then I went to Fairfield, Alabama to the First Baptist Church where I stayed for five years. After that, I was guided to Chattanooga, Tennessee, where I stayed forty years and six months in one church.

What I am saying is, I followed the guidance of God.

When our baby Joy died in 1946, that was the beginning of Camp Joy, where boys and girls begin to live. That has been an amazing place where literally hundreds and hundreds of boys and girls have gotten saved.

Then God put it on my heart to begin Tennessee Temple Schools.

Also, He led me to start Worldwide Faith Missions, supporting missionaries around the world.

I am trying to get you to see that God does guide each of us. Beware lest you forget His guidance.

III. THE BLESSING OF A GRATEFUL HEART

"But I have all, and abound: I am full, having received of Epaphroditus the things which were sent from you, an odour of a sweet smell, a sacrifice acceptable, wellpleasing to God."— Phil. 4:18.

Paul was grateful. Are you grateful that you are saved and going to Heaven? Are you happy that the Holy Spirit dwells in you? Are you happy to have a Bible that you can read and follow?

I'm afraid in this day and time we are not very grateful. Ingratitude is a sin. If you are guilty, ask God to help you be grateful for all He has given you.

Think back to the day when you got saved. You did not deserve to be saved, but God reached down and brought you out of darkness into light and gave you life everlasting. Be grateful for your salvation.

I was fourteen years old when I got saved. My mother and daddy were not saved and never went to church. In fact, none of us went to church. But I went to Sunday school with a friend, and the teacher, Miss Daisy Hawes, told me how to be saved. I can recall today just what she had to say about being born again. I listened, and one day on my knees in my home I said, "Lord Jesus, I now receive You as my Saviour." After all of these years, the fact of my salvation is unchanged. I am grateful for my salvation.

"But my God shall supply all your need according to his riches in glory by Christ Jesus" (Phil. 4:19). Are you grateful for His provisions for your needs?

Be grateful that He shows you what He wants you to do.

He guides us, step by step, day by day. You may not always understand or see what God is doing, but take your situation as from the Lord and be grateful.

When God called us to leave Fairfield, Alabama, where I spent five years, to come to Highland Park Baptist Church, the church here was divided. Many people were upset. Some things had gone wrong. In fact, it was a total mess when I got here. I preached for them, then I prayed much about being their pastor. I answered them that I would come. God gave me a direction for my life and ministry. I listened and obeyed.

Keep a grateful heart, a warm heart in a cold, critical day. This will make you be helpful and gracious toward others.

A grateful heart is a giving heart. Every child of God should be a tither, then give beyond the tithe.

When I got saved I began tithing, and I have kept it up all these years. God has never failed to provide for every single need.

I hope you will begin to tithe now, if you are not already doing so. You will be surprised how God will bless you.

A grateful heart is a concerned heart. You will have a concern for the lost. You will share the Gospel with others.

The Apostle Paul said, "For to me to live is Christ, and to die is gain."

IV. THE BLESSING OF A SURE FUTURE

Paul knew Jesus would come again. He believed the Christ who said, "I will come again," would do so. (Read John 14:1–6.) In Philippians 3:20 and 21 we read:

"For our conversation is in heaven; from whence also we look for the Saviour, the Lord Jesus Christ:

"Who shall change our vile body, that it may be fashioned like unto his glorious body, according to the working whereby he is able even to subdue all things unto himself."

Jesus is coming again. When, we know not. There will be a rapture, a snatching away of all the saved. The living will be changed, the dead raised, and we will meet Him in the air. That is the promise of the Son of God.

There is the promise of Heaven for all who trust Christ as their Saviour. There will be no separation, no sorrow, no more crying, no more suffering for all eternity. How wonderful to think of the blessing of a sure future! "I will come again, and receive you unto myself."

I graduated from the University of Louisville and majored in history. Then I went to a Southern Baptist seminary. I took three years of Greek from the famous A. T. Robertson. I had some of the finest teachers. In all of that, I knew nothing about the second coming of Jesus.

When I lived in back of the church at Greenbrier, Tennessee, I was alone. There was no phone to answer, and there was only a small congregation to preach to; so I began studying my Bible.

When I read John 14:1–3, where Jesus promised to come back for us, I saw the glorious truth of the second coming and began to preach it. I studied all the material I could about this matter and what would happen after His coming. I did not know about all the terms we use today, but I read on and believed God.

V. THE BLESSING OF A HOLY GOAL

"Brethren, I count not myself to have apprehended: but this one thing I do, forgetting those things which are behind, and reaching forth unto those things which are before,

"I press toward the mark for the prize of the high calling of God in Christ Jesus."—Phil. 3:13, 14.

Some people have absolutely no goal in life. Do you have a goal? Many are drifters. Both young and old need a goal, a God-honoring goal.

What is your goal? To make God first in your life? To read the Bible, pray and seek His face?

Then many have selfish goals—a bigger home, a newer car, money in the bank, designer clothes—on and on. People are money-crazy, popularity-crazy and selfish.

Many have sinful goals—to satisfy the flesh. That is why penitentiaries are full.

What is your goal? I have a goal. And at eighty-nine years of age, I am working at my goal every day.

Make a goal for your life. Keep separated from the world. Be doers of the Word. By your prayers that goal can be realized. By your testimony you are saying, "O God, I want to be my best for You. I want to honor You. I want my life to count."

Our text—Philippians 1:21–26—is from the Apostle Paul, a man in jail with a great heart, a singing heart and a rejoicing heart. He is rejoicing in the Lord.

In the midst of heartaches and sorrow, in times of temptation and trouble, ask the Lord for help, for guidance and for His blessing. Let Him use you to point others to the Lamb of God. Live so others will know that you belong to the Lord. You may be "peculiar," but praise God!

"For to me to live is Christ, and to die is gain" are words from a man in jail because of his faith. They too can be your song as you rejoice in the Lord, as you praise Him for all He has done for you.

Again, I say, let God use you to point others to our lovely Lord.

Sitting in my office one day, I looked out my window. Across the street I saw the house where my wife and I and family lived for many years. Down the sidewalk on that side of the street a big bulldozer went right up to the front door of that house, and in a few minutes the front was pushed down.

My mind went back to when we lived in that pastorium and to some things that had happened there. I thought of the night W. I. Powell, a deacon, came to my home and brought a lost man he wanted me to talk to. I opened my Bible and showed Bill Morgan the way of salvation. We knelt down in the living room and prayed, then he accepted Jesus as his own personal Saviour.

Bill Morgan was a drunkard, an alcoholic, a dope user, but God saved him. He is living for Christ today and serving Him in a local church. I see him quite often. I love this man of God. He has convictions.

Then, as I saw the house coming down, I thought of a fellow named Jowers. He came down Market Street, stopped in front of Union Gospel Mission, took out his knife and slashed his throat from ear to ear, then dropped over in the gutter right in front of the mission.

Police were called. They rushed him to the hospital. I went to see him in the emergency room. I stepped up beside him, lying there with blood everywhere, just a plain bum, with nothing in the world.

I said, "Mr. Jowers, can you hear me?"

The blood-soaked cloth fluttered at his throat, and I heard him say, "Yes."

I asked him if he was saved.

He said, "No, I know nothing about that."

I gave him the Gospel and told him that the only way to Heaven was through accepting the Lord Jesus Christ. After I had given him the way of salvation, I asked, "Sir, would you now at this moment receive Christ as your Saviour?"

He put out his hand and said, "Preacher, I will."

I had a prayer with him. Then I said, "If I don't see you again here on earth, I will meet you in Heaven," and walked out.

I preached in Highland Park four Sundays. On the fourth

Sunday, a fine, well-dressed man walked down the aisle, came up to me and said, "I have accepted Christ; I want to unite with the church. Do you know me?"

I said, "I don't believe I do."

"Oh yes, you do."

He leaned his head back, and across his throat was the scar where he had slashed himself with a knife from side to side. He reminded me that I was the man who led him to Christ in the hospital. "I was a drunken bum, and God has saved my soul. I want to follow my Lord in baptism and be a member of this church."

I baptized him, got him a room, and he was faithful to the church.

Then one day he came to me and said, "Brother Roberson, my wife divorced me some years ago. I lost my home, my two children—and everything. I don't blame her—I was a drunk then. I am going to Columbus, Georgia to see her. I want you to pray for me." We prayed and he left.

In a few days, I saw out my window a man coming up the sidewalk with a lady and a young lad by his side. They came to the door; he introduced his wife and one of his children. He said, "You led me to Christ; now will you lead my wife to the Lord?" They came inside, and I led Mrs. Jowers to the Lord in our living room. They got remarried and began living for God and serving Him together.

Are you ready to meet the Master? Do you know Christ as your Saviour? I am not talking about being a church member, being baptized, or any other works you might do. If you have not been saved, I pray you will settle it now. Make sure Heaven is your eternal home.

HOW TO FACE DISCOURAGEMENT

"Wait on the LORD: be of good courage, and he shall strengthen thine heart: wait, I say, on the LORD."—Ps. 27:14.

"Be strong and of a good courage."—Josh. 1:6.

I am talking about courage. Underscore that word in your Bible.

Discouragement comes to all. Some get discouraged more than others—some daily; some do not. Moses, Paul and John were discouraged at some time. So was David. Throughout the Psalms, he wrote about discouragement and his fight with it.

God bless you young folks! You get discouraged and disheartened. Sometimes your parents are not in favor of what you do.

The laboring man gets discouraged. So does the executive. Preachers get discouraged. Missionaries who get discouraged come back home.

The sick and afflicted get discouraged. So do old folks, and even successful people.

Still the Bible exhorts us, "Be of good courage." Keep your hopes up. Keep your faith in God.

Sometimes discouragement comes from opposition. When I left the Southern Baptist Convention in 1946, that stirred up some fire! There were articles in the newspapers about it. Many things were said. I had a rough time for a long time. However, I kept my faith in God. Since I knew God was with me and guiding me, I had no fear.

I became an independent Baptist, the only one in Chattanooga at that time. Today there are thirty-seven (or more) independent Baptist churches around the city.

I put up a very large tent on the Highland Park school ground across from the church for our revival meeting. (This was just a little after I had come out of the Convention.) One day I walked up to the tent. (It had curtains around the sides.) I heard voices. Inside were a number of Southern Baptist preachers. I heard one say that I may have come out of the Convention, but I would get tired of being independent and get back into the Convention.

Well, I am still out after all these years.

I have had opposition. And one can get discouraged when he has opposition.

Discouragement comes through finances and through physical, mental and moral difficulties. But strengthen your heart in God.

Discouragement comes through failure. When you feel that you have done your best but fail, you want to give up.

A preacher came to see me one Monday saying that he made an awful failure in his preaching the day before. Not one person came forward at the invitation, so at the end of the service he resigned. He said he had made a big mistake, and he had—the mistake of giving way to failure.

Keep on going. Keep trusting God.

A certain evangelist was a great friend, a good man. I had been with him in his church, and I had him in my church. He too gave way one night to discouragement. We were in a meeting in Springfield, Tennessee. He expected a thousand, but only a handful came. He was so discouraged. After he preached, he drove home, went straight in the house, opened the drawer, pulled out a revolver and killed himself. A great preacher, known by people everywhere, but he got discouraged.

The Word of God speaks on discouragement. No matter what it is—physical affliction, death of a loved one, a broken heart—come back to and wait on God.

We may get discouraged because a friend deserted us. Oftentimes they do. Look to the Lord for help. Continue serving Him.

What should we do when these hard, dark hours of discouragement come?

Come back to the One who is the same yesterday, today and forever! Don't forget God. You are in His family, and He is with you! When discouragement comes, say to yourself, *The Lord is here with me! The Lord never fails me. He will be with me through all my days. I have the Holy Spirit within to fill and empower me! I can go forward doing His will!*

Beware of certain things: all of us are still in the flesh, so we have the weaknesses of the flesh. We live in a sinful world. Discouragement is all about us. The Devil never stops working. Trouble abounds. But what do we do? When we have difficulties, when sorrows and heartaches come, what do we do? We come to God and say, "Lord, let not my faith fail."

Now if God be for us, who can be against us? Get committed to going on, to living for God.

The Bible is God's infallible, holy Word. I believe it from cover to cover. I can say that a little more emphatically than some of you might. I went to a Southern Baptist seminary. I took three years of Greek, finished the course with good grades. I listened to every criticism of the Bible, listened as

they laughed at the King James Bible. However, I maintained my faith in the Bible.

When discouragements and heartaches come, do you stay
with the Bible? Do you read it and rely on its promises?
Conditions change, people change, but the Bible remains
the same—God's holy, eternal Word!

For many years I had a favorite verse—I Peter 2:21: "For
even hereunto were ye called: because Christ also suffered
for us, leaving us an example, that ye should follow his
steps." Later, though, when God took from us a little one
(our baby Joy), God changed my life verse.

I was holding a big tent meeting in Russellville, Alabama
when I received the message that my baby was dead. As I
crossed the Tennessee River on my way home, God seemed
to change my life verse to Romans 8:28: "And we know that
all things work together for good to them that love God, to
them who are the called according to his purpose." And I
have been holding onto it ever since! That verse has seen me
through a thousand difficulties. I rest upon it in times of
discouragement.

When things go wrong, rely on the promises of God,
knowing that He never fails.

I suggest Psalm 23. I recommend Psalm 37. Let nothing
shake your faith!

In times of discouragement, get on your knees in prayer.

Satan trembles when he sees
The weakest saint upon his knees.

And I Thessalonians 5:17 tells us to "pray without ceasing." When in trouble, pray. When lonely, pray. When sick,
pray. When you fail, pray. When hours are dark, run to God.

Elijah was in trouble. The people of Israel had turned to
Baal. Two altars were built. Nothing happened to the altar
of Baal. But when Elijah prayed, fire came down on his
altar. Things happen when we pray.

Friend, make your choice: in difficult times or when enemies surround you, rely on the Word and power of God. When your heart is heavy and things are tough, look up to God. Seek His face. The fire fell when Elijah prayed, and fire will fall when you pray. Thousands of times I have prayed when things were dark, and I got the answer.

God led me to start Camp Joy for children when I had not a penny to put toward it. I prayed. Then when I heard about a hundred acres of land being sold out at Lake Chickamauga, I decided to check it out. I found they were selling it at a public auction in downtown Chattanooga. I went, along with a great big crowd of other people.

The auctioneer told about this beautiful land that was for sale. I sat way in the back of the building, longing for that property for Camp Joy, land where we could tell children about the Lord.

Once the floor was opened for bids, no one spoke. Finally I stood up and bid three thousand dollars. The auctioneer laughed at me. "That property is worth hundreds of thousands of dollars." I sat down.

He went on with the bidding. When he asked for bids, he got none.

Though he couldn't understand it, I did get the property.

He dismissed the crowd. When I walked up front, he told me he just couldn't believe that could happen. I told him I could—that I could explain exactly how it happened! He told me the property was mine for three thousand dollars.

Then I had to tell him that I didn't have any money, but if he would give me twenty-four hours, I could pay him.

I borrowed the money and paid him off. As a result, we began Camp Joy in 1946, and it has been running every summer, from June to August, since that date. The camp is free to children, and many thousands have been saved while attending.

When discouragement comes, trust God. Rely on His promises. He will see you through! In times of discouragement, when the night is dark, when things go wrong, when people are against you, when you are all alone, when you feel like you are fighting a battle, simply pray and wait on God! He never fails!

I have been discouraged many times.

In a big tent meeting up in Michigan, I spoke one night to a great assembly of people, and many were saved. I went to my hotel room for the night. When I awoke the next morning, I couldn't speak, couldn't make a sound. I knew nothing to do except write a note to the pastor that I couldn't preach, or even speak.

I left the meeting, went home and fought that battle for one year! I went to doctor after doctor, specialist after specialist. All said nothing could be done.

"You are through preaching," they told me. It was a dark, dark time.

I tried everything to get my voice back. Then after a year, suddenly God allowed me to preach again. I have been going ever since, trusting God every step I take!

When discouragement comes, read your Bible. When discouragement comes, pray. When discouragement comes, surrender to the holy will of God. Whatever may be your need, trust in the Lord.

I think of great men. I knew John R. Rice well. We were together hundreds of times in meetings. How that man prayed! I have heard him pray when I thought he would never finish. Oh, how God answered his prayers! He did mighty things through that one man, John R. Rice. I have seen the power of prayer.

So pray in your darkest hour. Pray yourself through every difficulty.

To win the battle against discouragement, come back to

God, back to His Book, back to your knees in prayer, and back to the work He has assigned to you. His command is still, "Go ye into all the world, and preach the gospel to every creature."

Has God called you to a definite task—to be a Sunday school teacher, a deacon, a leader or a soul winner? Then do what He says.

God gives courage to those who love and serve Him. When one is honest with God in the use of his time, money, giving and living, then he will have courage. God always blesses an obedient Christian. The blessings of God are on a witnessing Christian.

Happiness comes to those who trust God, love God and live according to His Word. In hours of pain, loneliness and failure, tell the Lord that you trust Him. Tell Him you will not quit, that you won't be guilty of turning away from His promises to this old world. Keep a song in your heart and be of good courage. "Wait on the LORD: be of good courage, and he shall strengthen thine heart: wait, I say, on the LORD" (Ps. 27:14).

Keep faith in God. Rest in the Lord. God will be with you in every trying hour.

I am trying to strengthen all Christians because within a few months some will be quitting, falling by the wayside because of discouragement. But, dear friend, in spite of your day-by-day difficulties, stay true to God!

In your battle for courage, don't complain, find fault or blame somebody else. Commit to loving and serving the Lord. Do your best for Him all the days of your life.

THE SEVEN RIGHT
BROTHERS

*"For the which cause I also suffer these things: nevertheless I
am not ashamed: for I know whom I have believed, and am persuaded that he is able to keep that which I have committed unto
him against that day."*—II Tim. 1:12.

Everyone in this audience knows the story of the Wright
Brothers, Orville and Wilbur. These men invented and built
the first successful airplane. On December 17, 1903, they
made the world's first flight in a power-driven, heavier-
than-air machine at Kitty Hawk, North Carolina.

Orville Wright piloted the plane. He flew 120 feet and
remained in the air 12 seconds.

The brothers made three more flights that day. The
longest, by Wilbur, was about 852 feet in 59 seconds.

Five, besides the Wright Brothers, witnessed the flights.
These men were the sons of a bishop of the United Brethren
Church. They had no idea of the worldwide implications of
that which happened on December 17, 1903.

When we speak about brothers, there are quite a few
interesting combinations in the Bible. For example, when
Samuel was trying to find a king for the people of Israel, he
looked at all of the sons of Jesse. Seven sons passed before
Samuel. But Samuel said, "The LORD hath not chosen

these." Finally David was brought in, and he was the one selected.

We have two famous brothers in a parable given by the Lord. This story is found in Luke 15—the story of the Prodigal Son. In this account, one son came to God with a right attitude of heart. The other, the elder son, became an objector and was rebuked by his father.

But we are not speaking of these sons in this message. I am thinking of seven words of instruction that I can give to young and old—seven important words.

I. BEGIN RIGHT

This is essential. All fails unless we begin right.

Begin right. Trust Christ as your personal Saviour. There must be no guessing, no "hoping so." There must be a positive "yes" on your part.

This is what the Apostle Paul had. From the day Jesus met Saul of Tarsus on the road to Damascus and Saul accepted Christ as his Saviour, Paul had a positive testimony for Christ. He could say, "For I know whom I have believed, and am persuaded that he is able to keep that which I have committed unto him against that day."

God is glorified by a positive testimony. Satan gains when a testimony is limp and hesitatingly given.

This was what troubled Elijah. In the days of King Ahab, the people were undecided about the two sides. They were on God's side for awhile, then on the side of Baal. When Elijah called the people together he asked, "How long halt ye between two opinions? If the LORD be God, follow him: but if Baal, then follow him."

Such a word as this needs to be said to people today.

Life begins with Christ! Therefore, one must begin right for his life to be successful.

A successful farmer, whose flocks and herds increased,

was wont to say to those who spoke to him about salvation, "I must make my fortune first. Then I shall attend to these matters."

One day he took suddenly ill and was driven home to lie on the bed, from which he never arose. To the one who sat by his side during the last hours of life and spoke to him often of spiritual things, he said in tones of bitter remorse, "I am a loser at last. I have gained the world, but I have lost my soul."

He died without a ray of hope. He passed from this life to stand one day before God to give an account of himself.

What does it profit a man if he gains the whole world and loses his own soul?

One of our newspapers this week had the story of a comedian who has been appearing in Chattanooga. He had stated that he had six million dollars. That's a lot of money, but his money is nothing if he does not know Jesus Christ. Without the Saviour, a man is a pauper.

Begin right!

II. CONTINUE RIGHT

Many profess to know Christ as Saviour; they openly identify themselves on the side of the people of God—but they do not grow. Listen to these instructions, these admonitions:

"But grow in grace, and in the knowledge of our Lord and Saviour Jesus Christ. To him be glory both now and for ever. Amen."—II Pet. 3:18.

"I press toward the mark for the prize of the high calling of God in Christ Jesus."—Phil. 3:14.

"Therefore leaving the principles of the doctrine of Christ, let us go on unto perfection; not laying again the foundation of repentance from dead works, and of faith toward God."—Heb. 6:1.

The Bible is filled with admonitions for the child of God; continue, grow in grace, move on.

This means to read the Bible daily. It is the world's only indestructible Book! When other volumes will have perished in the earth's coming renovation, God's Word alone will have been preserved. "Heaven and earth shall pass away, but my words shall not pass away" (Matt. 24:35).

Dr. Henry Grube was once talking about the Word of God in its power to comfort. He said that he heard a great preacher say, "More Christians rest on the promises of the 23rd Psalm than on any other passage of Scripture." He said another great saint of God was heard to say, "The 14th chapter of John is the place to go when you need peace and courage."

Grube commented, "These men were right because both passages of Scripture have proven to be a blessing to countless millions."

Henry Grube went on the say, "However, I have found Romans 8:28 to be a very soft pillow on which to lay one's head when the darkness comes and the fears abound."

He was right. I have found the same thing in my life. This verse has been a blessing to my heart: "And we know that all things work together for good to them that love God, to them who are the called according to his purpose."

"And we know...." Here is assurance. It is not a matter of guessing nor of hoping so. We can be sure.

"And we know that all things...." That means everything—great trials and small problems, difficulties and disappointments, heartaches, joy, success and failure.

"And we know that all things work together...." It removes all possibility of chance. God has a plan, a purpose, for each of His children. And He works events together to fulfill His program.

"And we know that all things work together for good...." All of our prayers may not be answered in the way we desire, but God will work things out for our good.

To continue right, there must be a reading of the Word of God.

To continue right, we must pray. Paul said, "Pray without ceasing."

To continue right, we must worship with regularity, not with a choice based upon our physical desire, but with the regularity which is established through faith in Christ.

One man said, "I pray some twenty-five times a day—as I walk, as I drive, as I work. And I guarantee that if a man will pray twenty-five times a day, it will change his life and the character of his thoughts."

This man continued, "I soak my mind with Bible passages. I have committed at least two hundred verses to memory and can say them over and over again to myself."

He then said, "I try to tell the Lord how much I love Him day by day. And I try to keep all sin out of my life."

Have some definite determination about giving your life and continuing in the way God would have you continue.

III. WORK RIGHT

Give attention to Psalm 84:10:

"For a day in thy courts is better than a thousand. I had rather be a doorkeeper in the house of my God, than to dwell in the tents of wickedness."

Yes, the psalmist is talking about working, about being "a doorkeeper." Work is important. The Saviour said, "I must work the works of him that sent me, while it is day: the night cometh, when no man can work" (John 9:4). Paul said, "Not slothful in business; fervent in spirit; serving the Lord" (Rom. 12:11).

Begin right, continue right, work right. Christians are to work.

First, it is our business to show forth Christ. If people are going to see Jesus in us, they must see that we have been in touch with our blessed Saviour.

Second, it is the Lord's command that we be witnesses: "Ye

shall be witnesses unto me." We must witness constantly and fervently.

Third, we must press upon others the need of Jesus Christ. There is a great danger that we will give our witness in such an indifferent way that we will fail to reach the hearts and minds of others. We must press the need of Christ upon the lost as we meet them, and upon the saved also.

Work right!

IV. PLAY RIGHT

"Whether therefore ye eat, or drink, or whatsoever ye do, do all to the glory of God."—I Cor. 10:31.

"Abstain from all appearance of evil."—I Thess. 5:22.

There is a place for recreation. Some people perform rather well in their Christian lives until they get to this point of "playing." It is then that they allow the world to drag them into forbidden paths. It is here that they dissipate their energies, destroy their influence, and besmirch the name of Christ.

We must love righteousness! Even in the matter of games, even in the matter of enjoyment, there must be a hating of evil.

One man said that we should start a hate campaign, saying there is far too little hatred for evil in the world.

He was right. We are too complacent about the evil of this day. Television, radio, newspapers, magazines, billboards, advertisements—all show evidence that men do not hate evil. Vulgarity, obscene remarks, filthy conversation—these speak of the lowness of man's mind.

Psalm 97:10 reads: "Ye that love the LORD, hate evil."

In Proverbs 6:16–19 we read:

"These six things doth the LORD hate: yea, seven are an abomination unto him:

"A proud look, a lying tongue, and hands that shed innocent blood,

"An heart that deviseth wicked imaginations, feet that be swift in running to mischief,

"A false witness that speaketh lies, and he that soweth discord among brethren."

The holy God hates all that is unholy, all that is contrary to His nature. Amos said we are to "hate the evil, and love the good."

Learn the secret of correct attitudes about recreation. Take a stand for God and refuse to compromise.

I had an experience when I was a teenager just two or three years after my conversion. The Sunday school class to which I belonged was having an evening of fun at the home of a Sunday school teacher. Someone suggested that we play Rook. I knew nothing about the game. Preparations were made, tables were put in certain positions, chairs were placed around them, then the Rook cards were brought out. At this time I noticed the Sunday school teacher went to the windows and began pulling down the shades. I asked why. She replied, "Well, someone may pass along the street and think we are playing cards. I don't want anyone to get a wrong impression. This is an innocent game. It is not gambling, but someone might misunderstand."

When she said that, I announced that I would not play the game. If there was any question about it that might be misunderstood by those on the outside, I would not participate.

This has been my general rule. I don't want to engage in anything that might have written upon it a question mark.

Many of you know the artistic works of Norman Rockwell. This famous artist said, "I have always wanted everybody to like my work, so I painted pictures that didn't disturb anybody, pictures I knew everyone would understand and like."

That rule might be good enough for painters, but it is a poor one for Christians.

Christians will always have some enemies. Some will always dislike what we believe and how we stand.

The recreation must be right!

V. PRAY RIGHT

For the sake of emphasis, let's repeat: begin right, continue right, work right, play right; now, pray right!

We have mentioned the matter of prayer already, but I would like to give it a special emphasis here.

Pray according to the Word of God. Pray in the name of Jesus Christ our Saviour. Jesus said:

"And whatsoever ye shall ask in my name, that will I do, that the Father may be glorified in the Son.

"If ye shall ask any thing in my name, I will do it."—John 14:13,14.

Establish definite prayer habits, like Daniel did. Bring every need before Him! Put away pride and selfishness, then seek His face for your every need.

Pray for guidance. This is important. Seek His face and pray for definite guidance.

Create a love for prayer, for it is from God that you receive the strength and power to do what is important in life. Ignore prayer, and you ignore the way for peace and accomplishment.

It is impossible to believe that one can be filled with the Holy Spirit unless he is one who prays. We want and need His fullness! Our lives are ineffective without the filling of the Spirit.

Many of our prayers should be: "O God, fill me with the Holy Spirit. Empty me of self and ready me for the fulness of the Spirit."

VI. SEE RIGHT

"Jesus saith unto them, My meat is to do the will of him that sent me, and to finish his work.

"Say not ye, There are four months, and then cometh harvest? behold, I say unto you, Lift up your eyes, and look on the fields; for they are white already to harvest.

"And he that reapeth receiveth wages, and gathereth fruit unto life eternal: that both he that soweth and he that reapeth may rejoice together."—John 4:34–36.

Do you see a world lost in sin? Do you see a world heading toward Hell? Do you see a world in need?

Seeing these will produce right giving. This will make a tither of every child of God. We are commanded:

"Bring ye all the tithes into the storehouse, that there may be meat in mine house, and prove me now herewith, saith the LORD of hosts, if I will not open you the windows of heaven, and pour you out a blessing, that there shall not be room enough to receive it."—Mal. 3:10.

Covetousness is one of mankind's great sins. Covetousness is back of dissension among nations. Covetousness was underneath the disturbance at the Olympic Games in Atlanta.

Christians who faithfully tithe are on the right road. Tithing not only is doing the right thing, but it also accomplishes much, and it brings special spiritual blessings to one's heart.

One day Abraham Lincoln was walking down the street with two small boys who were crying loudly. A neighbor passing by inquired, "What's the matter, Abe? Why all the fuss?"

Lincoln responded, "The trouble with these lads is what's wrong with the whole world. One has a walnut, and the other wants it!"

Watch your heart. Keep your life generous and obedient to your Master.

Seeing a world in need will not only produce right giving,

but it will also bring youth into missionary service. Young people, look at this world—lost in sin—and remember the words of Christ: "As my Father hath sent me, so send I you." Give your life to the cause of Christ and to the spreading of the Gospel. Volunteer for missionary service! Wait for God to give you direction for a field where He wants you to serve.

Again, seeing right will give all of us a concern for souls. We must see people as lost or saved. We must show our compassion for the salvation of sinners.

In the early years of Tennessee Temple, many things made indelible impressions upon me.

During the days of a missionary conference, excitement regarding missions increased. Young people were volunteering for mission fields.

A young lady student of our school came into my office one day and asked for a moment of my time. She sat down and began her conversation. Then as she said, "God has called me to be a missionary," she began to cry. When I asked her why she wanted to go to the mission field, through her tears she said, "Oh, they are lost! They are lost! They are lost! I must go and tell them of Jesus."

She did go, and for a number of years was a very successful missionary.

VII. DIE RIGHT

Begin right, continue right, work right, play right, pray right, see right; and now, die right!

Paul said, "I die daily" (I Cor. 15:31); "For ye are dead, and your life is hid with Christ in God" (Col. 3:3); "Likewise, reckon ye also yourselves to be dead indeed unto sin, but alive unto God through Jesus Christ our Lord" (Rom. 6:11).

First, die daily in order to honor Christ. Die to the positive and to the negative. Die to compliments and criticism. Self is your greatest enemy. When you die to self, then Christ is glorified.

Second, die daily in order to have peace and contentment. There is no mystery in this—all people want to have peace of heart. Jesus knew this. Paul knew it. Peter knew it. Hence, many words are given to us to tell us how we can be peaceful and contented.

Trouble is common, trouble is everywhere; but the Christian can have peace in the midst of trouble. Sweetly Jesus said, "Peace I leave with you, my peace I give unto you."

Emphatically the Apostle Paul tells us to come before God with "prayer and our supplication" and to know that "the peace of God which passeth all understanding shall keep your hearts and minds through Christ Jesus."

Young people in school, this is an essential lesson for you. There must be a reckoning of self to be dead.

Mothers and dads, this is a lesson for you also. Reckon self to be dead! Cease the search for your own ends. Find peace and contentment through trusting Him.

You will never have everything just as you want it. The world is full of disappointments. You will never be treated just as you feel you deserve to be treated. But you can still have peace. I know that what I am suggesting is difficult for the flesh, but we can have victory through our Saviour.

We had a fine Christian couple bring their son to Tennessee Temple Schools. Because of the crowds coming in, it was necessary to place the lad in a room which was not as nice as they would have liked and as we would have liked. Placing their son in this room was only temporary, but it upset the parents and, likewise, the boy.

The lad left school in a very short time. The parents have written back to us strongly critical, and they asked for a refund of the money which they had paid.

The refund was made. But it might have been better if they had said nothing at all. The actions of the parents placed into the heart of the lad a critical, self-seeking drive which may result in the wreckage of his spiritual life.

Die daily in order to have peace and contentment.

Three, die daily in order to bring forth fruit. Here is one of the sweetest verses in the Bible:

"Verily, verily, I say unto you, Except a corn of wheat fall into the ground and die, it abideth alone: but if it die, it bringeth forth much fruit."—John 12:24.

I want to be a fruit-bearing Christian. Do you? I want others to see Christ in me. Do you? I want to have the joy of leading souls to the Saviour. Do you? Well, this means death to self.

WHAT MAKES A GREAT CHRISTIAN?

"But so shall it not be among you: but whosoever will be great among you, shall be your minister:

"And whosoever of you will be the chiefest, shall be servant of all.

"For even the Son of man came not to be ministered unto, but to minister, and to give his life a ransom for many."—Mark 10:43–45.

"And I, brethren, could not speak unto you as unto spiritual, but as unto carnal, even as unto babes in Christ.

"I have fed you with milk, and not with meat: for hitherto ye were not able to bear it, neither yet now are ye able.

"For ye are yet carnal: for whereas there is among you envying, and strife, and divisions, are ye not carnal, and walk as men?"— I Cor. 3:1–3.

See the picture from this portion in Corinthians, written to the church—the people, their condition, and what God speaks to all of us about.

Think on this today: What makes a great Christian? What makes a really strong Christian? This is important because a sincere Christian wants to give his best to the Lord.

I got saved at age fourteen in Louisville, Kentucky. I was called to preach at age eighteen. I wanted to be in the house of God for Sunday school and all other times. I had determination.

Our desire today should be to give our best to the Lord. You are a new creature in Christ; you are born again; the Holy Spirit dwells in you; you have a New Testament church in which to worship and the call of God to reach out to others.

1. In listing some things that make a great Christian, I think of the word *faith*. "Have faith in God." First, there must be saving faith—knowing Christ as your Saviour. Then, there must be a living faith—day by day walking with Him. Paul said, "So then faith cometh by hearing, and hearing by the word of God" (Rom. 10:17).

Build your faith on the Word of God. Read the Bible and believe it. Build your faith on the Book.

Again, build your faith on personal experiences. Salvation is a miracle! I can't get over it, I shouldn't get over it, and I don't want to get over it. Daily use your faith to supply your needs and guide your every step. Build your faith by observing what God has done for others.

I think now of Charles Haddon Spurgeon, of George Mueller, of Praying John Hyde and others; I think of Peter, James and John—how God worked in all their lives.

Build your faith on the Word of God, not on man, nor newspapers, nor magazines, nor radio, nor television.

When I got saved at age fourteen, I went forward in a church on the edge of Louisville, Kentucky. The pastor was Rev. J. N. Benford. I didn't know it then, but he had been the pastor of a great, outstanding work, Emmanuel Baptist in Louisville. Now he was pastor of a little country church, Cedar Creek Baptist Church, where I got saved. He said, "I was led by the Lord to come here." This was a matter of his faith and honoring and trusting God in that decision.

2. A great Christian has rock-ribbed *convictions*. There is no greatness and there are no accomplishments without convictions from the Word of God.

The most important conviction is salvation through faith

in Christ. We must have convictions about separation from the world and living for Christ. We must have convictions about the local church and about missions.

I came to Chattanooga in 1942. After being here four years, God led me in something. We carried on this ministry until I felt we should be independent Baptists, completely separated from any convention. We had been Southern Baptists all through the years, but we decided to come out from that and be separated completely from it. I had a strong conviction on the matter.

I recall that a committee of five men were sent down from Nashville, men with Ph.D. degrees, to talk to me. We talked about an hour or two in my office. They told me I was making a big mistake. They felt I should get the church back in the Convention and stay there.

I listened, but I had convictions. I told them, "No, God has led us in what we are doing." And He had led us.

Out of the Highland Park Baptist Church have come hundreds of independent churches that are now doing a job around the world.

Without convictions we fail.

We had to have convictions on standards for our workers and teachers in the Sunday school. They had to sign a pledge to the fact of their salvation, that they would separate themselves from the world and be faithful and loyal.

3. The next word I want you to see as we think about being a great Christian is *vision*. There must be vision. "Where there is no vision, the people perish" (Prov. 29:18).

We must have a vision in winning people to Christ. There must be vision in the building of a local church and Sunday school. There must be a vision of world missions, a reaching out to the ends of the earth with the Gospel and pressing upon people their great need of salvation.

And you must have a vision of what God wants you to do.

Yes, people of all ages need a vision of what God wants them to do in this evil world.

I recall when God led me in starting Tennessee Temple Schools, beginning in 1946. I had prayed about it and definitely knew that God wanted me to begin this school. We had no money, no backing of any kind. But I believed God and believed He would take care of those things. And He proved Himself during all those years.

During my days there, hundreds were trained and went out preaching, witnessing, becoming missionaries on foreign fields and at home, and many Christians were using their talents in other areas for the glory of God.

Get a vision of what God wants you to do during your lifetime. Hear this:

Only one life; 'twill soon be past.
Only what's done for Christ will last.

With the one life you have, get a vision of what can be done.

Our baby Joy, a sweet little thing, died so suddenly. Our hearts were broken. But out of the death of our baby came Camp Joy for children. All of you know about Camp Joy. Again, God led me so definitely that we were to have this camp. I knew we would take children in, then win them to Christ, train them in Christian living and service. I felt led of God to start this camp even though we had no land nor any money. (Already I have given details of how God worked on our behalf.)

Ask God to give you a vision.

Art DeMoss, a stranger, came to me one day. He told me about getting saved up North in a tent meeting. He said he wanted to serve God, wanted to live for God every day and obey Him.

I asked Art if he felt called to preach. He said, "No."

"Do you feel led to be a missionary?"

He said, "No." Then he told me he thought God wanted him as a businessman, to make money and do things for God with it.

I said, "God bless you!"

I gave him a room upstairs in the old Temple building. He had no money, so I told the dining hall he was to eat free.

After a few days he walked in and said, "Preacher, I'm leaving. I got what I want. I now have a vision of what God can do with my life."

That man, Art DeMoss, became a multimillionaire. He gave Tennessee Temple thousands of dollars, and at his death left thirteen million dollars to the school.

What can happen when a person gets a vision from God, then obeys?

The words *faith, conviction* and *vision* are for the ones who want to be outstanding Christians.

4. There is another word: *endurance*. "Endure hardness, as a good soldier of Jesus Christ" (II Tim. 2:3). Nothing will be achieved without steadfastness. To endure, one must die to self. Paul said, "I die daily." He wanted to live for Christ.

Again, it means to be filled with the Holy Spirit. You have Him; now does He have you? If you are saved, you have the Holy Spirit. But does He have control of your life? You must tell God you want to be filled with the Holy Spirit, to be empowered by the Holy Spirit to do His work. This means determination. "This one thing I do...." You must have determination like Joshua, like Daniel, like Paul and like others. Enduring is not complaining nor murmuring, but doing with all your heart what God tells you to do.

5. Then to be a strong Christian, there must be *submission*: You need to say, "Father, Thy will be done." Some people say they can't know God's will. Oh yes, they can. God has a will for every one of us. Are you in His will? Are you doing His will?

What revelations would take place if we all knew and did the will of God!

Let God have His way! Be submissive to His holy will. Follow Him, love Him, serve Him and be what He wants you to be.

I read an old story about Henry Grady, editor of *The Atlanta Constitution* from about 1850 to 1879. He was one of the top men of the city. He grew weary and told the men that he was leaving.

He left and went to Rome, Georgia, to his homeplace. His father was dead, but his mother was still living. He came to her and said, "Mama, you led me to Christ, but now something is wrong. I am cold inside. I don't have any feeling. I am tired of the world. My business has worn me out. I have come back home so you can read the Bible to me and pray with me like you used to years ago." She did so. She read the Bible, and he listened.

Then he asked if they could do like they did years ago: after he got into bed, would she pray for him? She did exactly that.

This went on for a number of days. Finally he said, "Mama, I know where I'm going now. I'm ready to do God's will. I must go back to my work in Atlanta."

He went back a different man. He became famous.

To be an outstanding Christian, one has to be submissive. He doesn't fight. He doesn't struggle. He simply says, "Lord, I want Your will for my life, so I submit myself to You to use for Your glory."

Maybe God is calling someone now to full-time service. Does He want you to be a preacher, a missionary, a teacher or in some other service? Be submissive to His holy will.

While I was pastor of the First Baptist Church in Fairfield, Alabama, a committee came from the Highland Park Baptist Church in Chattanooga and said they were looking for a pastor. My ministry there at Fairfield had become a large church. For three years we had baptized more converts than any other Southern Baptist church in Alabama. Great things were happening, crowds were coming. A beautiful building was paid for. Everything was going great.

The committee asked me to come to Chattanooga. I did agree to go preach for them one Sunday but told them I was not interested in leaving Fairfield and was not concerned about being their pastor.

I drove to Chattanooga, went to Phillips Chapel (now Highland Park Baptist Church) and spoke on Sunday morning. It was a bitter-cold day, and just a handful of people were there. Nothing happened. I got in my car and started back home to Fairfield.

"That ends that," I said. I was not the least concerned. But I did tell the Lord, "Lord, I want Your will to be done."

The Lord spoke back to me: "I want you to go to Chattanooga."

I finally did accept the call and came to Chattanooga. I stayed forty years and six months as the pastor. Amazing things happened there, because I was in the will of God.

I was led of God to retire after forty years and six months. I had no idea about the future. But since my retirement, I have preached in more than seventeen hundred different churches, year after year, all over America and the world. I am thinking about retiring again!

6. What makes a great Christian? One more word— *compassion*. Jesus looked upon the people and had compassion for them. He cared, and we must care. Great Christians are compassionate and loving; they want others to be saved; they rejoice in the salvation of anyone brought to Christ. A compassionate person has a love for souls.

A man was beaten and robbed on Market Street in Chattanooga. He was left lying on the ground. He was calling for help, but the crowd was passing him by. No one stopped. No one cared. Finally, a policeman saw him and called for an ambulance. He was taken to a hospital. When I read the story, I went to the hospital. I wanted to talk to him.

I walked into the room. I saw his hands and face were bandaged. I asked him to tell me his story. He did.

"These two fellows beat me and knocked me to the ground, robbed me of my money, stepped on my hands and kicked me in the face. I screamed for help and kept calling out. People were passing me by. Not a soul came to help me. The two men walked away.

"Finally a policeman saw me and called for an ambulance. I was brought here." Then he added, "Brother Roberson, what's wrong with the world?"

The thing wrong is, people do not care. There is no compassion.

O God, give us compassion!

Compassion will change a lot of things. Compassion is generosity. There was a dear old deacon in the church at Greenbrier, Tennessee, where I was pastor for a number of years. He was gracious but as selfish as he could be. He gave one dollar per Sunday to church. He lived in a magnificent home, had tractors, wagons and trucks—everything needed for his business. But he gave one dollar per Sunday. I couldn't change his mind. "One dollar is enough," he said. Tithing didn't interest him. His heart was not moved.

Some other Christians get to that place. Ask God to make you generous.

Compassion means exemplary living for Christ, letting others see Jesus in you, living simply, as a child does. If there is a question about something, don't do it. If you are uncertain about something, then don't do it.

Compassion also shows concern for others, a real, heartfelt concern for men, women and children. Tell God you want to be what He wants you to be, that you want to keep people out of Hell.

I want to do my best to win people to our loving Saviour. God will use us when we let Him have His way. Let us pray for compassion.

These things should be in your life and mine: faith in Christ, love for the Word, compassion for souls, and submission to the Lord's will.

I had a ten-day meeting in a lovely church near Lakeland, Florida. The church was made up of well-dressed and dignified-looking people. When I stood to preach on the first night, right out in front of me was a poorly dressed and barefoot boy of about fourteen years of age.

After I had preached, the boy, with his bare feet sticking out in the aisle, stood up and walked down the aisle at the invitation time. (I thought to myself, *He's going home.*) But I was wrong. In a moment he brought with him a well-dressed young man. The barefoot boy said to me, "Preacher, he wants to be saved."

I turned to the fellow and asked if that were so. He said, "Yes, that's right." When I asked who had been talking to him, he pointed to the barefoot boy.

I led that young man to the Lord.

I was there for ten days in that meeting. Every single night that boy sat up in the front, barefoot and dressed in the same clothes. I learned that his mother and daddy were drunkards who lived in a trailer outside the town.

That boy had gotten saved and had heard the preacher say that a Christian should be getting people saved and getting them down the aisle of the church.

I watched that boy bring people every night.

Get the picture: a barefoot boy, fourteen years old, bringing people to Jesus. It was amazing to me.

I finished up on Thursday night. I had breakfast with the

pastor Friday morning in his home. A knock came at the door, and the wife opened it. She came back in a few moments with this boy who was carrying in his hand a brown paper bag. He walked up to me and said, "Brother Roberson, I have enjoyed the meeting so much. Last night when we took a love offering for you, I didn't have any money and couldn't give anything. But I did want you to have something to show you how much I enjoyed the meeting."

He pulled out of that bag a sackful of radishes. "I hope you will like these." I thanked him. He pulled something else out of the bag—a quart jar of dewberries that he had picked that morning. They were still moist from the dew. His ankles and feet were scratched from the briars.

My dear friend, that shows compassion.

If you are lost, please come to Christ today. If you want to be an outstanding Christian, tell God you want faith, convictions, vision, endurance, submission to His will, and compassion.

THE UNIVERSITY WE MUST ALL ATTEND

"Study to shew thyself approved unto God, a workman that needeth not to be ashamed, rightly dividing the word of truth."— II Tim. 2:15.

Whether we like it or not, we are going to school every day. We may fail or we may succeed, but we are going to school. Furthermore, there is no cessation of this. It lasts as long as life itself.

We are exhorted by the Word to study to show ourselves approved unto God. This is for every child of God.

We are also told to "shun profane and vain babblings: for they will increase unto more ungodliness."

It is evident from the epistles that Paul counted himself a student. He was always studying, always moving on, always striving to do better.

Now, let us see a few things that might help us as we go to school.

I. REQUIRED COURSES

In every college certain courses are required for every student. These will be English, history, science, mathematics, language and perhaps others. Each school will vary, but each school will have a list of required courses.

There are certain things that are required in this life. We may or may not like them. They are required just the same.

First, illness is a required course. With all diligence we may take care of these bodies, but at some time sickness takes hold of us. Sickness may come because of some failure, or it may come from someone else. Contagious diseases are prevalent among the strongest. You have had sickness at some time—this is a required course.

The Apostle Paul, one of the world's greatest men, had illness. He was afflicted with certain infirmities. He besought the Lord that these things be taken from him, but they remained. Instead, God gave him this word of encouragement: "My grace is sufficient for thee: for my strength is made perfect in weakness."

After such a word from the Lord, Paul said,

"Most gladly therefore will I rather glory in my infirmities, that the power of Christ may rest upon me.

"Therefore I take pleasure in infirmities, in reproaches, in necessities, in persecutions, in distresses for Christ's sake: for when I am weak, then am I strong."—II Cor. 12:9,10.

From the apostle we can certainly learn how we are to face the adversities of life which may come through illness.

Let every infirmity of the flesh bring you nearer to the Lord Jesus. Make each moment of suffering a medium for feeling His presence and submitting to His will.

Sickness reminds us that we are weak and frail. The strength of youth is soon gone. The weaknesses of middle and old age soon overtake us. Sickness is a required course.

Again, sickness reminds us that we are mortal. These bodies are given to suffering and, if Christ delays His coming, will come to death.

Second, hard work is a required course. A few are exempt, but the average person must apply himself diligently to daily work.

Of course, there are some like this assistant who was discharged from a certain business.

"Where is Sam?" asked an acquaintance.

The response was, "Sam doesn't work here anymore."

The friend said, "Do you have someone in mind for his vacancy?"

"Pshaw. When Sam left, he didn't leave a vacancy."

Some people do so little work, their leaving creates no vacancy. But work is a required course for all and should be engaged in with joy.

Our faith in God should never hinder us from exercising ourselves in diligent work. Some Christians give a false impression to the world. They emphasize faith but fail to say anything about works.

There is a legend of two knights who got into a dispute over the composition of a shield, which they saw flashing before a pavilion on a distant field. One declared that the shield was of gold, and the other vehemently asserted it was of silver. There was no occasion for a quarrel. Both were right, for each was looking on a different side of the shield.

So it is that faith is one side of the Christian's shield, and works, the other side. We are saved by faith in Jesus Christ, and because we are saved, we should enter into definite work for Him.

Third, a required course is day-by-day contact with others—in the home, in the school and in the business. We are to love them despite their unpleasant dispositions. We too are unpleasant to some. We must study how we can better live and work with others. This is a required course.

II. ELECTIVE COURSES

In every school there are some courses that can be chosen by the students. In life there are some things that are elective, and we can decide to take them or refuse them.

First, obedience is an elective course. You can be obedient or disobedient. God calls for your obedience. Make a choice.

Gideon had to decide whether or not to obey God. He put out the fleece and waited for God's answer. When he received it, he gave his full obedience to the Lord.

Daniel had to decide whether or not he would obey the Lord or follow the people around him. Daniel purposed in his heart that he would not defile himself with the king's meat and wine.

Jeremiah had to decide. It was not easy because many were opposed to the prophet, but Jeremiah made his choice to obey the Lord.

My friend, will you be counted as an obedient servant of Christ? Or will you follow in the steps of so many who are disobedient to the Saviour? I warn you: if you are disobedient, chastening will come. Just as all good parents chasten their children when they disobey, so must the Lord chasten His when they are disobedient. "For whom the Lord loveth he chasteneth, and scourgeth every son whom he receiveth" (Heb. 12:6).

Second, you choose the Lordship of Christ or the leadership of Satan for your home. It was Joshua who said, "As for me and my house, we will serve the LORD." The call comes to us: "Choose you this day whom ye will serve." A dedicated, beautiful home brings joy. A sinful, satanic home brings sorrow. What will you have?

Third, you choose to discipline your life or choose to live in sinful neglect. The Apostle Paul chose discipline.

One of my favorite portions of the Bible is I Corinthians 9:24–27:

"Know ye not that they which run in a race run all, but one receiveth the prize? So run, that ye may obtain.

"And every man that striveth for the mastery is temperate in all

things. Now they do it to obtain a corruptible crown; but we an incorruptible.

"I therefore so run, not as uncertainly; so fight I, not as one that beateth the air:

"But I keep under my body, and bring it into subjection: lest that by any means, when I have preached to others, I myself should be a castaway."

Strong Christians have chosen to discipline their lives. The way of sinful laxness brings loss. The way of discipline to the purpose of God brings joy and peace. Elect to take a course in obedience to the Saviour. Discipline your life and let Him have His way.

Fourth, every person faces the matter of sin. Will you hate sin or compromise with it? First, know that every sin is against God. Second, know that sin will hurt you. Sin hinders and keeps you from being what God would have you be. Hate sin for what it is and for what it does.

It is interesting to note that the first temptation in the history of the human race took place in a garden and with man at peace with the whole animal creation. The temptation of Jesus, the second Adam, took place in a wilderness where He was with wild beasts. That contrast between the first temptation and the temptation of Jesus—one in a garden, the other in a desert—is a picture of the ruin wrought by sin.

Fifth, elect today to give your devotion to Christ. This is your choice. You must either serve the Saviour or serve Satan. If you say, "I'll do as I please," then you are following after Satan. If you say, "I can make my way—I need no help," then you are walking in the pathway of evil. You may be sincere about it, you may feel that you are doing right, but this will not change the matter of your transgression.

At the time of the Boxer uprising in China, some of the Boxers did not believe that they could be killed by bullets.

They thought their incantations and strange rites made them invulnerable.

These men were very honest and entirely sincere in this belief, but a Chinese army officer demanded they prove their sincerity by drawing up in a line so his soldiers could shoot at them. They immediately consented, for they were very sincere.

They drew up in a line and fearlessly faced the firing squad. The Chinese soldiers blazed away, and the Boxers dropped dead. Their doubt of the power of bullets that killed them did not alter the fact.

You may be sincere in your selfishness and in your disobedience, but that does not change the fact.

There must be devotion to Christ, or there will be slavery to Satan.

III. GRADUATION

In every school, college or university, there will be required and elective courses. Graduation belongs to the ones who complete the work and fulfill all graduation requirements.

But for you—you are coming to the completion of your work. The day of graduation will soon be upon you. You may dislike it, and you may fight against it, but it is coming.

"It is appointed unto men once to die, but after this the judgment."—Heb. 9:27.

If Christ tarries, death is coming. If Christ comes, we must meet Him, then comes the judgment.

For the Christian, there is coming the judgment seat of Christ. Listen to the Word of God:

"For we must all appear before the judgment seat of Christ; that every one may receive the things done in his body, according to that he hath done, whether it be good or bad."—II Cor. 5:10.

"Every man's work shall be made manifest: for the day shall

declare it, because it shall be revealed by fire; and the fire shall try every man's work of what sort it is.

"If any man's work abide which he hath built thereupon, he shall receive a reward."—I Cor. 3:13, 14.

My Christian friend, the day of judgment is coming, the day when you will be judged for your works and for your service. If you are found faithful, you will receive a reward. If you are found unfaithful, you will suffer loss. You will be saved, yet so as by fire.

But there is coming also a judgment for sinners. They will come one day before the great white throne judgment. The sinner stands there as a lost man, condemned for Hell. The judgment will tell how great will be his punishment.

"And I saw a great white throne, and him that sat on it, from whose face the earth and the heaven fled away; and there was found no place for them.

"And I saw the dead, small and great, stand before God; and the books were opened: and another book was opened, which is the book of life: and the dead were judged out of those things which were written in the books, according to their works."— Rev. 20:11, 12.

We shudder as we think of the torment and punishment which will come upon those who have rejected the Saviour.

I want you to see how serious a matter it is to reject Christ. Your eternal soul is at stake.

You have but one soul. Give it to God! "Believe on the Lord Jesus Christ, and thou shalt be saved."

You have but one life. Give it to God! Let Him use your life in a way that will bring blessings, especially salvation, to others.

You have but one great opportunity to serve God; therefore, do it while you can.

It was Dr. R. A. Torrey who told of a godly old man with a worthless son. That son was far more anxious to make money than he was to do right. He determined to go into a wicked business in which there is much money, but which no self-respecting man will undertake—the liquor business.

(Any man who is willing to make money from selling rum, whether legalized or bootleg, is willing to coin money out of the tears of brokenhearted wives, out of the groans and sighs of drunken sons and daughters, out of the heart's blood of their fellowmen, for this infernal liquor traffic is sending thousands every year to premature graves.)

This young man opened a saloon. His father was ashamed and brokenhearted. He pleaded with his son to get out of the business. But the son, bent on making money, wouldn't listen to his father.

The day came for the opening of the saloon. The father was among the first ones on hand. He stood outside, and every time a man approached the door, he stepped up and told him of the misery that came from strong drink and warned of the consequences of entering such a place. One after another the customers turned away.

The son wondered why he had no customers. Looking out the window to see if he could find the reason, he saw his own father turning customers away.

In great rage he came outside and said, "Father, go home! You are ruining my business."

The father replied, "I cannot help it, my son. I won't have my name dishonored by this business. And if you are bent on going on with it, I'll stand here and warn every man who approaches not to enter your door."

Finally the son lost control of himself and struck his aged father. The father turned to him without the least anger and said, "My son, you can strike me if you will; you can kill me if you will; but no man shall enter your saloon unless he goes over my dead body."

My friend, don't spurn the call and the wooing of God. Jesus died upon the cross for your salvation, and if you go to Hell, you will have to go over the crucified Son of God. He is ready to save you now if you will repent and believe on Him.

We are going to school—every one of us. Some courses are required, and some we may choose to take, but we are coming to the end of life when we must stand before God.

Are you ready to meet Him?

14

"JESUS WEPT"

"Then when Mary was come where Jesus was, and saw him, she fell down at his feet, saying unto him, Lord, if thou hadst been here, my brother had not died.

"When Jesus therefore saw her weeping, and the Jews also weeping which came with her, he groaned in the spirit, and was troubled,

"And said, Where have ye laid him? They said unto him, Lord, come and see.

"Jesus wept.

"Then said the Jews, Behold how he loved him!"—John 11:32–36.

"Jesus wept." The Son of God—God incarnate in human flesh—wept. Hold these two words in your thinking.

I read a story about a missionary who had heard of the death of a seventeen-year-old boy. He went to the home where the body lay. It was packed and jammed, with people standing around outside. The missionary knew these Indonesians were heathen; and all were standing around weeping, with no hope.

The missionary said, "I think God is crying over the loss of this soul who knew not the Saviour, and crying for the family who has no hope in God. And these people who mourn—they have no hope."

This story got next to me, especially, "I think God is crying."

I believe we are here tonight by the hand of God. You are here because God is alive, you are alive, and He brought you to the house of God on this Sunday evening. But I think God is crying at the conditions today and the things that are going on.

He is the eternal God, yet Jesus wept over the death of Lazarus, then raised him from the dead. Jesus walked upon the earth, then died upon the cross to save lost sinners. We see the compassion of God, the love, the concern of God.

Does Jesus care? Oh yes, He cares. His heart is touched with my grief. Does Jesus care? Yes, Jesus cares enough to die for sinful man.

I marvel that people can get so far away from God. I marvel that people can ignore God when He has done so much for us. He lets us live and breathe and be here to have fellowship with one another. Yet we fail to recognize the hand of God.

I think He is crying because we ignore Him, we pay no attention to His Bible, and we don't pray as we should. People are crazy about money, prestige, power and being big shots. Washington is full of them. Your town and my town are full of them. People have gotten away from God.

God is crying over physical giants of our day who pay no attention to Him—giants in basketball, football, baseball and all other sports. They are put on television as giants in the athletic world, but they completely ignore God. I think God is crying about that.

God is crying over the financial greats who ignore Him. The millionaires, the wealthy and near-wealthy turn to their riches and away from God. God is crying over them.

The pleasure-loving people, the pleasure-mad multitudes of the world, the nightclub crowd, drinking, wicked and sinful—God is crying over these.

God is crying over the educational wizards who ignore

Him. They may have doctor of philosophy degrees and other doctoral degrees from big schools where they ignore God altogether. God knows they have forgotten Him and are ignoring Him.

"Jesus wept." When we see God's concern over a lost and dying world, we should have at least some compassion.

We ignore God's Word. We do not read it every day. We do not pray as we should and claim God's promises. He said if we ask anything in His name, He would do it. Oh, we pray when we feel like it or get in a tight squeeze. God cries over our prayerless lives.

God is crying over our lack of faith. Jesus said, "Have faith in God." But I am afraid God cries because we exhibit no faith. We demonstrate no faith. We would rather worry. We would rather tell the psychologist about our troubles.

I think God is crying over our failure to witness for Him. Jesus said, "Ye shall be witnesses unto me," yet many Christians never witness. God cries over that.

God is crying over our neglect of worship. Praise God for all who are here, but all around are churches that are empty for Sunday night and Wednesday night services. Many had to close their doors because people quit coming.

I think God is crying because so many of His children are not growing in grace. When a person gets saved, he is to read his Bible and grow daily and keep on growing.

God is crying over our love for the world. People love the world and the things of the world. See the picture as given to us in the Bible. God cries over sinful mankind. He sees our sins, our disobedience, our stubbornness, our weaknesses, our unbelief, our selfishness, our blindness to truth.

Be careful, my friend, that you don't trample the love of God under your feet. Be careful that you do not ignore God. Don't give Him cause to weep over you as Jesus wept over the death of His friend Lazarus. Be careful to be concerned for others.

God is a God of love, patience and long-suffering. He loves you and cares for you. You are saved tonight only by the grace of God. You are somebody because God loves you. Don't forget that.

Remember this brief outline:

I. THE CHARACTER OF GOD

"And we have known and believed the love that God hath to us. God is love: and he that dwelleth in love, dwelleth in God, and God in him" (I John 4:16). This is the character of God. "For God so loved the world...." His love sent Jesus to die for us.

His love sent the Gospel to my ears as a fourteen-year-old boy in Louisville, Kentucky (my second year of high school). I knew nothing of the Bible, of Christ and salvation; but the Lord reached down, gave me the message and saved my soul.

His love has given us the Holy Spirit. We are never alone. We have had Him since the day of our salvation, to empower, to guide, to direct and to comfort us.

His love gives the promise of eternal life.

His love gives us daily access to His presence through our prayer life and fellowship with Him.

Any one of us can bring sorrow and heartache to the heart of Jesus because He loves us, He weeps over us, and He is concerned about us. Our personal God is so real that any one of us who is saved by grace can bring sorrow to His heart when we fail Him and ignore Him.

II. THE CONCERN OF GOD

I base this on Matthew 9:36:

"But when he saw the multitudes, he was moved with compassion on them, because they fainted, and were scattered abroad, as sheep having no shepherd."

Without Christ, men are lost and going to Hell. There is only one Saviour. He said, "I am the way, the truth, and the life: no man cometh unto the Father, but by me." Man is condemned already without Christ: "But God commendeth his love toward us, in that, while we were yet sinners, Christ died for us."

What an amazing fact, that the eternal God, the Maker of this whole universe, so loved us—you and me—that He Himself would let His Son die upon the cross so we could have life everlasting!

But I believe God is crying because some of His own are not living as they should—not serving Him, not praying, not going to church, not winning souls as they should. Many are simply failing in so many areas.

In the Saturday paper in Chattanooga a few weeks ago was a big headline: "Hell—What Is That Infernal Place Really All About?" The article mentioned a book by C. N. Kelly and Rosemary Rogers, entitled *Who Is in Hell? A Guide to the Whole _____ Bunch,* a book that sells for $12.95, by Warner Press.

What kind of a person could write such a book? Someone who ignores the Bible, ignores Christ, the cross, the blood of Jesus, and drags His name down into the dust, then laughs about it.

Hell is real! Without Christ, people are lost and will spend an eternity in Hell. Christ died for you. He loves you and will save you now and give you life everlasting. But Hell is a place of Christ-rejecters, a place for those who have turned their backs on the Son of God.

Salvation is a personal matter. I cannot do it for you, nor can your pastor or your family. You yourself must receive Jesus for your own remission of sins. You cannot ignore His shedding of blood for you.

III. THE COMMAND OF GOD

We are commanded to go into all the world and proclaim the message of salvation.

"Go ye therefore, and teach all nations, baptizing them in the name of the Father, and of the Son, and of the Holy Ghost:

"Teaching them to observe all things whatsoever I have commanded you: and, lo, I am with you alway, even unto the end of the world. Amen."—Matt. 28:19,20.

We have no alternative. We must obey and go after those who are lost. The wages of sin is death. We must be urgent and go for souls. Since Satan is busy deceiving the whole world, we must be missionaries. We must be witnessing and sending missionaries to the uttermost parts of the world so others can hear the Gospel and be saved.

The command of God:

"But ye shall receive power, after that the Holy Ghost is come upon you: and ye shall be witnesses unto me both in Jerusalem, and in all Judæa, and in Samaria, and unto the uttermost part of the earth."—Acts 1:8.

We must go because men are lost. Put aside all human reasoning, and tell people about Christ.

I was visiting in a home. A little mother said, "I don't want you bothering my boy. You don't need to talk with him about the church, about the Bible, for he is a good boy." No, he is not! He is a lost sinner. Every person without Christ is lost.

"He that winneth souls is wise." We are to obey that command and be witnesses for the Lord. I see some, not many, good soul-winning programs in churches. Some are reaching out to the ends of the earth.

The time is short, so we must go. We must go, for death is near to everyone. We are all living inches and seconds from death. We must go because the second coming of Christ is real! He said, "I will come again." So we must tell the gospel story while there is time.

I think God is crying. I know He is concerned. I know He loves us.

God is concerned that we let Him have His way with us, that we live so that we glorify Him.

I want to be found faithful when the end of my life comes or when Christ returns. I want nothing to hinder me from doing my best. I don't want God weeping over something in my life that displeases Him. I don't want to step aside into the shadows. I don't want to do that which is doubtful or questionable. I want to live for Him every hour. I want His name to be glorified. I want Christ to be seen in my life. I want so to live for Christ that people will know He is my Saviour, my Lord, my Master. I want my life to be lifting up others that they might see Christ and know Him, so they will be saved.

I have dealt in this message with a personal thing—God's concern for us. His tears are for us.

If you are not saved, will you tell the Lord, "Lord Jesus, I want You as my Saviour. I want You as my Master. I want to know You as my Friend. I want to receive You right now into my heart"?

May God grant it!

THE FINE ART OF CRITICIZING

"For even hereunto were ye called; because Christ also suffered for us, leaving us an example, that ye should follow his steps."—I Pet. 2:21.

The aim of everyone should be to be Christlike. Since we have been redeemed by His blood, we should seek to be like Him.

To be Christlike, we must know Him: how He came from God, was born of a virgin and lived among men; how He lived, preached, taught, loved, died, rose again, and how He ascended back to the Father; what He thought about sin, about life and about death.

Then we must know ourselves: what we are—our strengths, our weaknesses, our failures, our successes. Then we must know what we have in Him. We are new creatures, indwelt by the Holy Spirit.

We must know how to live victoriously: "This is the victory that overcometh the world, even our faith." Yes, and we must know others—their strengths, their weaknesses and their needs.

Someone said:

> I looked upon my brother with the microscope of criticism and said, "How coarse my brother is!" I looked at him with the telescope of scorn and said,

"How small my brother is!" I looked into the mirror of Truth and said, "How like me my brother is!"

We are discussing "The Fine Art of Criticism."

I have a few choice statements which I give to critics: "Critics are a dime a dozen." I use that statement to indicate the value that I give to the professional critic. (Some are "professional." They spend a lifetime criticizing others. Rarely do they see their own faults but are quick to pick out the faults of others.)

Another statement: "Any fool can criticize, and most of them do."

Think on these things:

We must not seek criticism; it will come to us all. Abraham Lincoln said, "He has a right to criticize who has a heart to help."

We must not compromise to avoid criticism. Some fear criticism and will change their lifestyle to avoid it. Young people will drop their good standards to avoid the laughing critics of the world.

We must not refuse the lessons of criticism. There are some lessons to learn if we are wise.

First, there can be profit from criticism. Criticism can help you. You may not like it, but it opens your eyes to yourself.

Singers can profit from criticism—they can become better singers. Preachers can profit from criticism—they can be better preachers.

Southern Baptists had a strong critic for many years in J. Frank Norris, an independent and pastor of the First Baptist Church of Fort Worth, Texas. He wrote his criticism of the Convention in *The Fundamentalist*. He spoke his criticism of the Convention from every platform of the nation. He attended almost every Southern Baptist Convention and held a counter-rally in some nearby auditorium. He attacked modernism in the Convention, especially in the schools and among the leaders. He exposed the spending of money for what he called worthless causes.

Southern Baptists did not like Norris, but many leaders say he helped the Convention. His criticism opened their eyes to things that were happening, especially the teaching of evolution at Baylor University.

Second, there can be loss from criticism. Discouragement may come to a sincere heart from some evil or thoughtless critic. Preachers have become defeated by critics.

The one man who meant so much to my young ministry was Rev. L. W. Benedict of Louisville, Kentucky. He was pastor of Parkland Baptist Church. He had brought into his home a young man, had sent him to school and had paid his bills. But the young man listened to the critics of the pastor.

One morning he arose in the congregation of the Parkland Baptist Church and said, "I make a motion that the pulpit of this church be declared vacant." The shock of this happening almost caused the death of the pastor. He spent weeks in the hospital. This remained with him for a lifetime.

Critics can harm you!

Third, learn when to ignore criticism. Paul did. Especially ignore criticism that turns you away from obeying the Bible.

I am a fundamentalist! I believe the Bible from cover to cover. Some critics call me a "liberal." If I were weak in faith, it might turn me away from fundamentalism. But being what I am, I ignore criticism!

Ignore criticism that minimizes sacrificial service. People may criticize your service for Christ. They may advise, "You are doing too much"; or "Take it easy"; or "Give less of your time"; or "Let others do some of the work." Ignore such criticism, such advice.

Ignore criticism that diminishes your zeal. Young people get on fire for God, then some wiseacres criticize and laugh at them. Ignore such critics. Go on spending yourself in Christian service. (Even parents will sometimes criticize their children for their zeal.)

Ignore criticism that laughs at faithfulness. The world calls you a fanatic when you go to church faithfully, when you tithe, and when you have a family altar. Keep on with what you are doing.

Ignore criticism that weakens your convictions about His Word, about Christian living and about soul winning.

Be Christlike! Have the spirit of Christ.

I. WE MUST HAVE HIS HATRED FOR SIN

He loved sinners but hated sin. In His prayer in John 17:15, Christ said, "I pray not that thou shouldest take them out of the world, but that thou shouldest keep them from the evil."

In John 3:20 we read, "For every one that doeth evil hateth the light, neither cometh to the light, lest his deeds should be reproved."

If we love Christ, we will hate sin. Strong drink, immorality, indecency, gambling, profanity, gossip—all are sins. Too many of us are too lenient toward some sin in which we indulge. Some hate liquor or profanity but give way to gossip or neglect being faithful in church attendance.

II. WE MUST HAVE HIS UTTER DISLIKE FOR HYPOCRISY

The open declaration of our Lord is given in Matthew 23. His strongest words were delivered to the Pharisees as He viewed their hypocrisy, calling them hypocrites, blind guides, fools, whited sepulchers, murderers, serpents and a generation of vipers.

As you think of His hatred for hypocrisy, you must read His cry over Jerusalem in Matthew 23:37:

"O Jerusalem, Jerusalem, thou that killest the prophets, and stonest them which are sent unto thee, how often would I have gathered thy children together, even as a hen gathereth her chickens under her wings, and ye would not!"

Oh, the love of Christ for sinful men! But oh, His hatred for hypocrisy!

III. WE MUST HAVE HIS LOVE FOR RIGHTEOUSNESS

Christ complimented generosity. Read about the widow's mite in Mark 12:41–44. She gave *all!* Would He compliment your giving?

He complimented unselfishness. In Mark 2:1–12 is the story of the four men bearing the palsied man to Christ. Jesus complimented their unselfishness.

He complimented faith. In Matthew 15:21–28 we read of the woman bringing her daughter to Jesus. The disciples tried to send her away. She persisted. Jesus' compliment to her was, "Great is thy faith."

To face this world of critics (enemies of God), we must die to self.

"Verily, verily, I say unto you, Except a corn of wheat fall into the ground and die, it abideth alone: but if it die, it bringeth forth much fruit."—John 12:24.

Last night in Maryland a man thanked me for a message on death to self which I had given in Pennsylvania. He said it changed him, his home and his Christian service.

We must die to self!

We must center our thinking on Christ, the fairest of ten thousand. He never disappoints us.

The minds of millions are fixed on earth's problems; consequently, they are disturbed and nervous. I urge you to center your thinking on Christ, who is "the same yesterday, and to day, and for ever."

We must remember the eternity of the soul. Let nothing turn you from a passion for the souls of men. Souls are eternal! Heaven is eternal! Hell is eternal!

This above all—we must be Christlike! We must seek souls!

16

THE HAPPIEST MOMENT OF MY LIFE

"And I said, What shall I do, Lord? And the Lord said unto me, Arise, and go into Damascus; and there it shall be told thee of all things which are appointed for thee to do."—Acts 22:10.

On May 27, 1972, Donahue won the Indianapolis 500 race. As his expensive race car came to a stop and the microphone was shoved in front of his face, he said, "This is the happiest moment of my life!"

I appreciate his enthusiasm for his work and his joy in accomplishment. But if winning a race creates the happiest moment of his life, he has had a very drab and dull life! But this statement has often been made.

The jockey who won the horse race at Churchill Downs in Louisville, Kentucky said, "This is the happiest moment of my life!"

An opera star, a fine and talented soprano, said when she finished a difficult but delightful opera, "This is the happiest moment of my life!"

When a striving young man was elevated to a good position in his company, he said, "This is the happiest moment of my life!"

I am not criticizing them for their exuberance in accomplishment. We should be excited about our work and rejoice in our achievements.

But is there an experience that can be called the happiest of all? I believe there is. Salvation is certainly the greatest and the happiest experience of life. Whether it be the salvation of Mel Trotter, a drunken bum, or a sweet young child of ten years, it is the greatest and happiest experience one can ever have.

Keep in mind that we are talking about salvation, not an empty profession. Many make professions but have no evidence of knowing Christ as Saviour. It is not for us to judge, but Jesus said, "By their fruits ye shall know them."

Quite often in conducting a funeral service, I search for some good word that will bring encouragement to the family. A number of times I have had people say to me, "Mr. So-and-so was not a church man. He had not gone to church in years, but he did make a profession when he was a boy."

I have sincere doubts about people who make professions of faith, then do nothing about it.

So, when I speak about the happiest moment of my life, I speak of that moment when I came to know Jesus Christ as my Saviour.

The Apostle Paul counted his salvation experience as the happiest moment of his life. He delighted to recount his experience. He told of his sin of persecuting Christians. He told of his journey toward Damascus and the bright light which shined round about him. He told of hearing the voice of Jesus. Then he recounted what he said to the Lord: "Lord, what wilt thou have me to do?" (Acts 9:6).

According to the Bible, what must man do in order to come to this, the greatest experience of life?

First, he must hear the Gospel. Romans 10:17 tells us, "Faith cometh by hearing, and hearing by the word of God." It doesn't matter where you hear it or how you hear it, but you have to hear it. It may be from a Sunday school teacher or from an eloquent evangelist, but the Gospel must be heard—the "Good News" of salvation.

Second, he must be convicted of sin. There must be the knowledge that you are a lost and undone sinner and that salvation can come only through Christ. That conviction comes from the Holy Spirit.

Third, he must be repentant. Repentance is godly sorrow for sin. We must see that our rejection of Jesus Christ is the most heinous of all sins.

Fourth, he must accept Jesus Christ as personal Saviour. Jesus said, "He that heareth my word, and believeth on him that sent me, hath everlasting life" (John 5:24).

Again, I must say, salvation is instantaneous. The very moment one repents and believes in Jesus Christ, he becomes a child of God, and his name is written down in the Lamb's book of life. It is not a matter of working and waiting; it is a matter of repenting and believing.

Now, it is my contention that the happiest moment of life is the moment of salvation. Let me tell you why.

I. SALVATION IS GREAT BECAUSE OF TIME

By one single act of life, you become the possessor of everlasting life.

"Verily, verily, I say unto you, He that believeth on me hath everlasting life."—John 6:47.

"For the wages of sin is death; but the gift of God is eternal life through Jesus Christ our Lord."—Rom. 6:23.

"He that hath the Son hath life; and he that hath not the Son of God hath not life."—I John 5:12.

Life is yours through Christ, the Son of God. The Bible establishes three definite things:

First, salvation is the *gift* of God. Paul said, "Not by works of righteousness which we have done, but according to his mercy he saved us" (Titus 3:5). Paul again said, "For by grace are ye saved through faith; and that not of yourselves: it is the gift of God: Not of works, lest any man should boast" (Eph. 2:8,9).

Second, salvation is the *eternal* gift of God. I do not know of any way to describe eternity.

They say that in the olden days, some of the preachers, in trying to tell the length of eternity, would liken this world to a great steel ball and say, "Suppose an eagle were to swoop down once every one hundred years and barely touch the steel ball with his beak. When the world-sized steel ball is completely worn out, eternity will just be beginning."

Or one of the old-time preachers might say, "Suppose a sparrow took a drop of water in his beak from the Atlantic Ocean, then hopped across the United States and deposited that drop in the Pacific Ocean. Then suppose he hopped back across the country for another drop from the Atlantic and kept repeating the process. When the sparrow emptied the Atlantic into the Pacific, eternity would have just begun."

These are simple illustrations, but they might help someone to see what we have in Christ. Salvation is an eternal gift!

Third, salvation is the *blessed*, eternal gift of God. We have life in Christ now, but we have life forevermore. We have the promise of Heaven. How blessed will our heavenly life be! There will be no pain, no trouble, no problems, no tears; and remember, this blessed life is eternal.

How blessed to be redeemed by the precious blood of the Lord Jesus Christ!

Dr. A. J. Gordon was pastor for many years in Boston, Massachusetts. One day he met a little boy out in front of the church carrying a rusty birdcage in his hands. Several little birds were fluttering around in the bottom of the cage.

Dr. Gordon asked, "Son, where did you get those birds?"

The boy answered, "I trapped them out in the field."

The preacher said, "What are you going to do with them?"

The boy answered, "I'm going to take them home and play with them, have some fun with them."

Dr. Gordon said, "What will you do with them when you get through playing with them?"

The boy replied, "I guess I'll just feed them to an old cat we have around the house."

Then Dr. Gordon asked the boy how much he would take for the birds.

The boy answered, "Mister, you don't want these birds. They are just little old fieldbirds, and they can't sing very well."

Dr. Gordon said, "I will give you two dollars for the cage and the birds."

The boy said, "All right, it's a deal. But you are making a mistake." The exchange was made, and the boy went whistling down the street with two dollars in his pocket.

Dr. Gordon took the cage out behind his church, opened the door, and the birds went soaring away into the blue sky.

The next Sunday Dr. Gordon took the empty birdcage to the pulpit to use as an illustration in his sermon. He told his congregation about the little boy and what had happened to the birds. Then he said, "That little boy said that the birds could not sing very well, but when I released them from the cage, they went singing away into the blue. And it seems they were singing, 'Redeemed! Redeemed! Redeemed!'"

Salvation is great because of time: we are redeemed for eternity.

II. SALVATION IS GREAT BECAUSE OF THE TRANSFORMATION OF LIFE

What miracles are wrought when men come to the Lord Jesus Christ!

"Therefore if any man be in Christ, he is a new creature: old

things are passed away; behold, all things are become new."—
II Cor. 5:17.

Man is a sinner and separated from God by his sin. We
have no way of measuring the wreckage and waste of life
caused by sin.

Reformation fails! Resolutions fail! Regeneration alone
can transform a life!

This happiest moment gives the knowledge of salvation.
We can know that we have "passed from death unto life."

This happiest moment gives the Saviour's peace. Jesus
said, "Peace I leave with you, my peace I give unto you: not
as the world giveth, give I unto you. Let not your heart be
troubled, neither let it be afraid" (John 14:27).

This happiest moment gives God's direction. Following
self can lead into desperate circumstances, but following the
Holy Spirit will guide us into fields of service.

Mrs. J. M. Dawson was a talented Sunday school teacher.
In her class was a young woman who had two outstanding
talents: a marvelous singing voice and the gift of helping
others, especially children.

One day the young lady came to Mrs. Dawson's home and
announced, "I am going to be a grand opera singer. My
father is sending me away to study. Someday I am going
to be a star, and my name will be in bright lights on
Broadway."

Years went by. One day Mrs. Dawson was speaking in a
Southern city. This young woman came up to her. "What are
you doing now?" Mrs. Dawson asked.

The young lady replied, "I am the head of a hospital for
crippled children."

Mrs. Dawson said, "What about your music?"

The girl answered, "One day I went to a missionary society to sing. Afterward a woman spoke who had been on the
mission field for thirty years. Her hair was gray. Lines of

suffering showed on her face. As she spoke of her work, I thought to myself, *Surely she can retire now. She won't go back over there.* But soon she said, 'I must go back and live for those for whom Christ died.'

"When I heard that, I thought of my puny, selfish efforts. God spoke to me that day. I went back to school, took a nursing course, and I am now running this home for crippled children."

Later Mrs. Dawson went out to the home for crippled children and walked from room to room and bed to bed with this girl, this would-be opera singer. Her compassion for the children was outstanding. She said to Mrs. Dawson, "I would rather have the privilege of helping these children than to be the greatest prima donna in the world."

If you follow God's direction, if you are submissive to His leading, He will show you what to do.

Something else you can have in this transformed life is God's power, the power of the Holy Spirit, to do His work.

It may seem to some that I am painting extravagant pictures. But those of you who know the Saviour can testify that all of these things are true. Salvation brings us peace, direction and power.

III. SALVATION IS GREAT BECAUSE IT MAKES YOU A CHILD OF GOD

"The Spirit itself beareth witness with our spirit, that we are the children of God:

"And if children, then heirs; heirs of God, and joint-heirs with Christ; if so be that we suffer with him, that we may be also glorified together."—Rom. 8:16, 17.

Rejoice that you can sing:

I'm a child of the King, a child of the King:
With Jesus my Saviour I'm a child of the King.

First, you are indwelt by the Holy Spirit. Jesus said, "And I will pray the Father, and he shall give you another Comforter, that he may abide with you for ever" (John 14:16). When you received Jesus Christ as your Saviour, the Holy Spirit came in.

Second, you have been given an understanding of the Word of God. This Book is a closed Book to the natural man, for "the natural man receiveth not the things of the Spirit of God" (I Cor. 2:14). But for the child of God, there is an understanding of the Bible. The Holy Spirit illumines its pages for us.

The Holy Spirit is the key to the Word of God. When you have a key, you can open a door and enter in. The Holy Spirit also opens the pages of the Bible. He gives light to your mind and heart as you read and study.

Third, you have the right to pray. Through faith in Jesus Christ, God is your Father. Now you can pray, "Our Father which art in heaven...."

You need not bear your burdens alone. You can cast your cares upon the Lord, for He cares for you.

Fourth, you will be with God forever. Many wonderful things are to take place in the future. Christ is coming, and you will be caught up to meet Him. You will reign with the Saviour for a thousand years upon this earth. You will be brought into the new heavens and new earth by the power of God. All of these things are yours through Christ.

Some of you may be saying, "I'm saved, but I don't have this happiness." Some of you may be confessing that you had happiness at your conversion but it has not continued.

Let me give some simple suggestions:

First, recognize that Christ lives within. The Apostle Paul says in Galatians 2:20, "Christ liveth in me." Each day be conscious of the very presence of the Saviour.

Second, rejoice in the Holy Spirit's leadership. He will guide you, so wait on Him.

Third, repeat the story of your conversion. Don't be a secret disciple, as Nicodemus was. Be as the woman of Samaria, who went everywhere telling what Jesus had done for her. Be as the Apostle Paul who, at every opportunity, delighted to tell the story of his conversion.

Fourth, tell the story of salvation to the whole world.

A man boarded a train in Chicago. Soon a short, stocky man came in and sat down beside him. When the train pulled out of the station, the man who had gotten on last pulled out a Bible and read it for awhile, then closed it and said to the other man, "Beautiful day, isn't it?"

The other man agreed that it was.

"There are some fine crops in this section of the country."

"Yes, some very fine crops."

"God is good to give these people such fine crops, isn't He?"

The other man did not reply.

The Bible-believing man said, "You didn't reply. Aren't you a Christian?"

"No, Sir."

So the Bible-believing man read to him a few verses of Scripture and said, "Why not bow your head on the seat right now and let me pray for you?"

In telling about it later, the other man said, "Before I knew it, I had bowed my head. The man's arm was around me, and he was praying for me. When I lifted my head, I was a saved man! I had invited Jesus to come into my heart. When we arrived at the station and he started out, I remembered that I did not know who he was. I rushed to the door and shouted, 'What is your name?' He answered back in one word, 'Moody.'"

Mr. Moody believed in passing the word along.

Some of you may be thinking that I painted an extraordinary picture of salvation. As a matter of fact, the picture has been a very ordinary one. There is much more that could be said about this great matter. But I trust that I have said enough to make some of you want to be saved; for, above all, you need Christ as your Saviour. He is the door to life now and forever. Christ is life!

Go to the funeral parlor. Look into the face of the young man who lies in the casket. He has two hands, but he cannot use them. He has two feet, but he cannot walk. He has two ears, but he cannot hear. He has two eyes, but he cannot see. He has a mouth, but he cannot speak. What does he lack? The breath of life.

Today you may have everything from the standpoint of the world. But without Jesus Christ, you lack the one thing which is the greatest of all—salvation.

There is one beautiful verse that I want you to hear:

"But as many as received him, to them gave he power to become the sons of God, even to them that believe on his name."—John 1:12.

To be saved, you must receive the Lord Jesus Christ.

When Andrew Jackson was president of our United States, a man by the name of Wilson was condemned to die for a crime he had committed. The governor of his state issued this man a pardon, but he refused to accept it, saying, "I don't want the pardon. I don't want to live." The governor insisted that he take the pardon, but Wilson insisted that he didn't have to receive it.

The case was taken all the way to the Supreme Court. The Court decreed that Wilson did not have to accept the pardon, that a pardon was of no value unless a man was willing to receive it. So Wilson died.

God is offering you a pardon. He is offering you salvation, but you must receive it.

AN APPEAL FOR COURAGEOUS SERVICE

"Therefore, my beloved brethren, be ye stedfast, unmoveable, always abounding in the work of the Lord, forasmuch as ye know that your labour is not in vain in the Lord."—I Cor. 15:58.

Everyone is aware of the broad scope of knowledge of the Apostle Paul: a man of thorough education, trained to be a rabbi, a leader, a spokesman for the people of Israel.

Solomon has been called the wisest man who ever lived. His words were wise; his decisions were right. Yet Solomon played the fool by turning away from God and worshipping idols. God became angry with him (I Kings 11), and He took away his power and leadership.

This did not happen to Saul of Tarsus. He turned to Christ and joined the people he once hated. He became the chief spokesman for Christ, the Saviour. Paul remained true to the end of his life. There was no blemish on his record. Hear him as he speaks:

"For I am now ready to be offered, and the time of my departure is at hand.

"I have fought a good fight, I have finished my course, I have kept the faith:

"Henceforth there is laid up for me a crown of righteousness,

*which the Lord, the righteous judge, shall give me at that day: and
not to me only, but unto all them also that love his appearing."*—
II Tim. 4:6–8.

As we look at our text in I Corinthians 15:58, the first
word stops us: "Therefore." What had Paul been saying?
What led him to that final sentence?

In this great chapter, Paul touched the heights.

1. He revealed his own faith. He believed in the crucified and risen Saviour. "Christ died for our sins according to
the scriptures."

**2. He placed before mankind the truth of the res-
urrection.** The apostle said, "And if Christ be not
risen...your faith is also vain....and ye are yet in your sins."
Christ arose! We shall arise from the dead.

Last Wednesday I stood on a windy hillside and said the
final words over the grave of one of our members. As I looked
at the gravestones in that country cemetery, I remembered
that Christ is coming back, the dead in Christ will arise, and
we shall be changed. We shall meet our Lord in the air.

3. Paul said that Christ is coming: "Behold, I shew
you a mystery; We shall not all sleep, but we shall all be
changed." The resurrection and the translation!

4. Then Paul took aim at death: "O death, where is thy
sting? O grave, where is thy victory? The sting of death is
sin; and the strength of sin is the law." Now watch: "But
thanks be to God, which giveth us the victory through our
Lord Jesus Christ."

Was that Paul's conclusion? NO! He gave a "therefore." In
the light of all that he gave us in I Corinthians 15, he said,
"Therefore, my beloved brethren...."

I. BEHAVIOR

"Therefore, my beloved brethren, be ye stedfast, unmoveable." After a stirring proclamation of great truth, Paul

talks to the individual Christians of Corinth. He was not discussing doctrines, but living—behavior. He was not discussing baptism, the Lord's Supper, eternal security or the second coming, but behavior. "Be ye stedfast, unmoveable."

The Corinthians were sinful and shifting—in line one day, out of line the next.

Be steadfast, unmovable, in life. Be steadfast, unmovable, in faith. Be stedfast, unmovable, in testimony.

"Be ye stedfast, unmoveable":

(1) In convictions. "Stand therefore." Don't be swayed. Don't be overpowered by the world, but "stand therefore" in this dirty, filthy world.

(2) In daily life. Live for Christ. Don't change; don't compromise! See the importance of life, the power of influence.

(3) In prosperity. Be steadfast! Many fail in prosperity. They turn away from God. Moses pointed out Israel's problem.

(4) In poverty. When need overwhelms you!

(5) In suffering. When pain strikes, when you face the worst.

(6) In sorrow. When loved ones are taken from you. Be steadfast, unmovable!

Are you glorifying God by your behavior? Are you showing forth Christ by behavior?

II. SERVICE

"Always abounding in the work of the Lord."

Always abounding—not quitting. Always abounding—not complaining. Always abounding—not shirking your obligation.

(1) Serve willingly, not grudgingly. "If I do this thing willingly, I have a reward."

(2) Serve unselfishly. Forget self. "For all seek their own, not the things which are Jesus Christ's."

(3) Serve lovingly. Love is the desire to serve.

(4) Serve faithfully. "Be thou faithful unto death."

"Always abounding in the work of the Lord." What is that work?

It is not building buildings. It is not operating colleges. It is not running a business. It is not conducting a bingo party.

"The work of the Lord" is witnessing. The Great Commission is given in the Gospels and in Acts: "Ye shall be witnesses unto me" (Acts 1:8). Tell others of Christ.

"Always abounding in the work of the Lord." Abounding! Enthusiastically abounding! Serving happily. "Abounding" in what? Telling the happiest news ever committed unto man. What do we tell? "Christ died for our sins according to the scriptures."

All of us must abound! *All* of us must witness! *All*—not just a few, but all.

III. REWARDS

"Forasmuch as ye know that your labour is not in vain in the Lord."

(1) Rewards now for soul-winning labor.

A lady said, "Do you remember me? You led me to Christ forty years ago." I did not remember her, for she was just a child forty years ago. But I did get great joy out of seeing the result of witnessing.

Enter into that work. There will be rewards. Oh yes, you may have some closed doors and some harsh words, but there is JOY in soul winning!

(2) Rewards later—at the judgment seat. Christ is coming, and one day we shall stand before Him to give an account of ourselves.

"For we shall all stand before the judgment seat of Christ."— Rom. 14:10.

"So then every one of us shall give account of himself to God."—Rom. 14:12.

"Every man's work shall be made manifest."—I Cor. 3:13.

He will not overlook anything. He will not forget the slightest work done for Him. *He* will not forget. You will be rewarded.

(3) Rewards for eternity.

"Do ye not know that the saints shall judge the world? and if the world shall be judged by you, are ye unworthy to judge the smallest matters?

"Know ye not that we shall judge angels? how much more things that pertain to this life?"—I Cor. 6:2, 3.

The saints shall judge the world. How thrilling!

Another verse that presents a picture for eternity is I John 3:2:

"Beloved, now are we the sons of God, and it doth not yet appear what we shall be: but we know that, when he shall appear, we shall be like him; for we shall see him as he is."

We shall be like Him. Many of our sick and shut-ins now will have new bodies then.

IV. CHRIST IS THE NEED OF MAN!

Ole Bull, the great violinist, and John Erickson, the great inventor, were good friends as boys. Then years and careers separated them. In America they met again. Ole Bull invited his friend to come hear him play in a concert. John Erickson said, "I have no time for music. I have work to do."

Ole Bull offered to come to his shop and play for him, but John refused.

Then Ole Bull thought of a way: Go to John with a supposed problem of sound. This he did.

Erickson took the violin apart and put it back together. Then when Ole Bull drew the bow across the strings, there were marvelous, sweet tones.

Ole Bull played a great favorite. Everyone in the shop stopped. Men came and stood in wonder. The beauty of the music entranced them.

Finally, when Ole Bull stopped, John Erickson lifted his bowed head, revealing his tears. With reverence he whispered, "Play on. Don't stop. I never knew before what was lacking in my life."

I present to you Christ! How much you miss without Him! He is what you need! Make Him your Saviour! Make Him first in your life!

APPROACHING THE DEADLINE

"And it came to pass, when the time was come that he should be received up, he stedfastly set his face to go to Jerusalem."—
Luke 9:51.

Life is composed of a series of deadlines.

During Reagan's presidency, the air controllers went on strike for more money and additional benefits. The president gave the strikers a deadline: 11:00 a.m., August 5. Striking government men were to be back at their work by that hour or be fired. They lost their jobs!

Deadlines are common.

Newspapers operate on deadlines. Day-by-day news is printed by a certain time.

Schools operate on deadlines. There are cutoff dates for enrollment, cutoff dates for financial payment, and cutoff dates for examinations.

Governments operate on deadlines.

Businesses operate on deadlines.

There are deadlines in graduation. There is commencement night. Your work is finished; your diploma is handed to you; you have finished your course. There is the tossing of hats upon graduation.

There are deadlines in retirement. A man works to a

certain date, fulfilling his promise to his employer, then retires.

Men in the armed services of our country work on a deadline.

There are deadlines in life! Death comes. "It is appointed unto men once to die, but after this the judgment."

If Christ delays His coming, there is a time when all of us come to a deadline—a step over the line into the presence of our God. "Absent from the body...present with the Lord."

I repeat, life is a series of deadlines. (The derelict, the bum, may escape some deadlines, but one he cannot escape is the deadline of death.)

The greatest illustration on "Approaching the Deadline" is Christ. He steadfastly set His face to go to Jerusalem, toward the cross.

First, the cross was on His mind. "To this end was I born, and for this cause came I into the world, that I should bear witness unto the truth. Every one that is of the truth heareth my voice" (John 18:37).

Second, the cross was in His teaching. "Yet a little while, and the world seeth me no more" (John 14:19). In verses before that, He was instructing His disciples before approaching His deadline—His death on the cross.

Third, the cross was in His prayers. He prayed, saying, "Father, if thou be willing, remove this cup from me: nevertheless not my will, but thine, be done" (Luke 22:42). In the Garden of Gethsemane, He agonized in prayer as He prepared for the cross. The cross was the deadline! There Christ died for our sins!

But there was another deadline—His resurrection. He had already told His disciples He would arise in three days. And He did!

Then another deadline was His ascension. The time was fixed. He met His disciples. He gave them the Great

Commission, then ascended back to the Father!

There is another deadline—the second coming of Christ. *When* is in the hands of the Father. Jesus said, "But of that day and hour knoweth no man...but my Father only" (Matt. 24:36).

To approach the great moment of life successfully, certain things are essential. These are the things that make life meaningful and worthwhile.

I. SALVATION

This is essential. There are **no** substitutes for salvation, and it is available to everyone. "Whosoever will may come."

Salvation brings you into the family of God, and it makes available all the promises of God.

A remarkable strength is imparted to us when we can say, "We are the children of God." It matters not whether we are facing life or death; we can face it better when we know Him. Salvation helps us face the ordinary deadlines of life.

II. DEDICATION

Paul says in Romans 12:1,2:

"I beseech you therefore, brethren, by the mercies of God, that ye present your bodies a living sacrifice, holy, acceptable unto God, which is your reasonable service.

"And be not conformed to this world: but be ye transformed by the renewing of your mind, that ye may prove what is that good, and acceptable, and perfect, will of God."

Paul asked Christ on the Damascus road, "Lord, what wilt thou have me to do?"

Salvation and dedication should come together, but they seldom do. They did with Paul.

Dedication encompasses three things: the will of God— knowing and doing His will; death to self—reckoning self to be dead; the fullness of the Holy Spirit—giving power for every work of God.

III. SUPPLICATION

To approach any great moment of life, prayer is mandatory. You cannot face life without being equipped with prayer. God's great people have always prayed when approaching strategic moments.

Moses prayed. It is written of him, "And Moses besought the LORD." On his 120th birthday he talked with God, and God told him some things that would happen to the people of Israel. God gave Moses a song to sing to the people. (Read Deuteronomy 32.)

Elijah prayed on that dark, foreboding day on Mount Carmel. The prophets of Baal were there. The backslidden children of Israel were there.

Paul prayed. "And at midnight Paul and Silas prayed" at Philippi (Acts 16:25).

Peter prayed. "Peter went up upon the housetop to pray" (Acts 10:9). As he prayed, God caused him to see the need of the Gentiles.

Our Saviour prayed! On the eve of the crucifixion, He prayed in the Garden of Gethsemane.

The disciples prayed at Pentecost. They did not know the greatness of Pentecost, but they prayed in preparation.

Jesus said, "And, behold, I send the promise of my Father upon you: but tarry ye in the city of Jerusalem, until ye be endued with power from on high" (Luke 24:49).

All of life can be enriched and strengthened by prayer. Prayer will make things right when the deadline comes.

IV. SUBMISSION; ACCEPTANCE

To approach any great moment, let there be submission or acceptance. Seek His will. Know His will. Accept His will.

Paul's greatness began when he accepted God's will for his life. God's will led to sufferings, and God's will led to glory.

Submission is more than singing "Have Thine Own Way" or "Where He Leads Me I Will Follow."

Submission is pictured in Christ: "Father...thy will be done." Submission to the Father brings happiness to us now and hereafter. Submission to the Father gives usefulness to one's life.

A girl came to her high school graduation with great joy. After graduation, she went for a ride with her boyfriend. He had a bottle of liquor, and they drank it. There came a car crash, and she was killed! The deadline for her had come. That story has been repeated over and over: drunk driving—a crash then death.

Approach the deadlines of life with salvation, dedication, supplication and submission.

19

DON'T WASTE YOUR SORROWS

"He is despised and rejected of men; a man of sorrows, and acquainted with grief: and we hid as it were our faces from him; he was despised, and we esteemed him not.

"Surely he hath borne our griefs, and carried our sorrows: yet we did esteem him stricken, smitten of God, and afflicted.

"But he was wounded for our transgressions, he was bruised for our iniquities: the chastisement of our peace was upon him; and with his stripes we are healed.

"All we like sheep have gone astray; we have turned every one to his own way; and the LORD hath laid on him the iniquity of us all."—Isa. 53:3–6.

"Verily, verily, I say unto you, That ye shall weep and lament, but the world shall rejoice: and ye shall be sorrowful, but your sorrow shall be turned into joy."—John 16:20.

The Lord Jesus was a man of sorrows and acquainted with grief. Christ was not a man of jokes, but a man of sorrows. If we are to be Christlike even in the slightest way, we must understand something of His heartbreak.

February 26, I read in the devotional book compiled by Mrs. Charles Cowman, "Sorrows are too precious to be wasted." Then on March 5, I was given a book entitled *Don't Waste Your Sorrows*, by Paul Billheimer.

Mrs. Cowman said she got her thought from Alexander

Maclaren. He reminded God's people that sorrows will, if we
let them,

> Blow us to His breast, as a strong wind might
> sweep a man into some refuge from itself. I am sure
> there are many who can thankfully attest that they
> were brought nearer to God by some short, sharp sor-
> row than by long days of prosperity.
>
> Take care that you do not waste your sorrows, that
> you do not let the precious gifts of disappointments,
> pain, loss, loneliness, ill health, or similar afflictions
> that come into your daily life mar you instead of mend-
> ing you. See that they send you nearer to God, and not
> that they drive you farther from Him.

Someone has said, "The world's greatest blessings have
come out of its greatest sorrows."

Another has said, "We owe much to suffering. Many of
the richest blessings that have come down to us from the
past are the fruit of sorrow and pain."

The Word says, "Our light affliction, which is but for a
moment, worketh for us a far more exceeding and eternal
weight of glory" (II Cor. 4:17).

First, there is the sorrow of death. "Death is the
world's most crowded freeway." Death is the common experience of humanity. All must die—thousands do every hour.

We speak of death as a departure; Heaven sees it as an
arrival. We call death a hooded specter; Heaven sees it as an
angel of light. We call it separation; Heaven calls it reunion.
We call it a grave; Heaven calls it a gateway. We say "good-
bye" here, but it is "good morning" up there.

The sorrow of death should draw us nearer to His side.

There are blessings in the sorrow of death that God
wants you to have.

Second, there is the sorrow of a broken body. Illness
is everywhere. No one is exempt. For a little time, some may
feel they have escaped—but not for long. I have seen the big,

strong and husky brought to the sickbed. I have seen the vigorous and athletic reduced to the use of a cane or a wheelchair.

I read a magnificent story from *The Saturday Evening Post* of March 1981. It is the story of Paul Herbert Davis. At seventy-nine years of age, he made his first parachute jump. At eighty he made another parachute jump. He is now eighty-three years old. He keeps two secretaries busy eight and ten hours per day.

He has worked with some of the great leaders of America. But he is disturbed by the conviction that America is declining. He believes that the energy, commitment, vision, virtue and determination that pushed this nation to the top are on the wane.

But all has not been easy for Mr. Davis. He has had fourteen operations, four of them for cancer.

This man is saying to many, "Don't waste your sorrows of a broken body."

Third, there is the sorrow of disrupted plans. Sometimes health causes plans to be changed. Sometimes finances cause plans to be revised. Sometimes because of world conditions, plans have to be changed.

President Ronald Reagan had his plans disturbed by the wild bullet of a deranged young man.

Don't waste your sorrows on disrupted plans! God has a purpose in it all. "All things work together for good to them that love God" (Rom. 8:28).

I have a book with the listing of all my special meetings in different cities. It goes back for thirty-five years. But there is one blank year. No meetings! I was on the shelf from October 1972 to September 1973. I didn't waste my sorrows on those twelve months.

Fourth, the sorrow of tragic failure. We regret failure. We are disturbed by our failures. But wait! Don't waste your sorrow! It may be that hardship is the only way God can train you for what He wants you to do. Sometimes He has to work through a broken heart, a broken body, a tragic failure.

The world aims for success. It seems to be the god of most people—in the financial world, the entertainment world, even the church world.

Failures awaken us. They cause us to see what is important. So don't waste your sorrow on failure. God may use it to do His work and bless your life.

Now, we note some lessons:

I. LET ALL THINGS PRESS YOU TO HIS SIDE

Paul's thorn in the flesh—we do not know what it was— illustrates our lesson. He prayed for deliverance, but it remained. God's answer was, "My grace is sufficient for thee: for my strength is made perfect in weakness."

With that answer, Paul said:

"Most gladly therefore will I rather glory in my infirmities, that the power of Christ may rest upon me. Therefore, I take pleasure in infirmities, in reproaches, in necessities, in persecutions, in distresses for Christ's sake: for when I am weak, then am I strong."— II Cor. 12:9, 10.

Don't waste your sorrows. Let things press you to His side.

II. LET ALL THINGS INCREASE YOUR SPIRITUAL STRENGTH

Where is peace in tragedy? in sorrow? in sickness? in death?

Peace is not in music, not in concerts, not in symphonies.

Peace is not in movies, nor in television, nor in dancing, nor in debate, nor in education.

Peace is not in drinking, in immorality, in profanity, nor in lying.

Peace comes from the Man of Sorrows. Peace comes from the Christ who wasted no time with foolish jokes and trivial actions. Christ said, "My peace I give unto you."

III. LET ALL THINGS GLORIFY HIS NAME

A little German couple in Fairfield had lost all. They came to our home, and I led them to Christ. They rejoiced. They glorified His name! Losing all had brought them to Christ. Losing all brought the greatest joy they had ever known.

Let all things glorify His name.

IV. LET ALL THINGS OPEN YOUR HEART TO OTHERS

In sorrow, in tragedy, in dark hours, we become self-centered. We pity ourselves! Don't waste your sorrows! Let such things open your heart to *others*. Let your sorrows give you an understanding of *others*. All have troubles. All seek for someone to help.

You have pain of body? Your Saviour understands. He endured the pain of the cross.

You have been mistreated by others? Our Saviour understands. Men forsook Him. They drove nails into His hands and feet.

You are having money problems? He understands. He wants you to know that He has all you need. "But my God shall supply all your need" (Phil. 4:19).

You are passing through a night of sorrow? He understands. He is "a man of sorrows."

Don't waste your sorrows. Let everything draw you to Him—your tears, your fears, your loneliness, your weakness, your burdens.

THE CHRISTIAN AND
THE FUTURE

"Behold, I have set the land before you: go in and possess the land which the LORD sware unto your fathers, Abraham, Isaac, and Jacob, to give unto them and to their seed after them."

"Behold, the LORD thy God hath set the land before thee: go up and possess it, as the LORD God of thy fathers hath said unto thee; fear not, neither be discouraged."—Deut. 1:8,21.

The Bible emphasizes the importance of today. It is today that a man must decide about Christ. It is today that a man must make his decision about following God or following Baal. It is today that we are exhorted to surrender our all.

Why the constant emphasis on today? Simply, we know not what the morrow may bring. James tells us, "For what is your life? It is even a vapour, that appeareth for a little time, and then vanisheth away" (Jas. 4:14). Therefore, we can see the importance of today.

But at the same time, the Bible has a constant emphasis on the future. The cry, "Prepare to meet thy God," is given in a hundred ways in this infallible Book. There is coming a time when we must meet God! 'Prepare for it,' says the Word.

In Deuteronomy, Moses spoke to the people of Israel about the future. They were ready now, after forty years of wandering, to cross into the Promised Land.

Enemies would face God's people. Strong cities would stand against them. Discouragement would dog their footsteps. Fear would fill their hearts. But Moses said to them, "Go on. God is with you. The land is yours."

The people went in, conquered the inhabitants and possessed the land. As long as they obeyed the words of Moses, they had success. When they disobeyed his words, they failed.

The lesson is a good one for us. When we follow this Book, we succeed. When we don't follow its teachings, we fail.

Now let us consider "The Christian and the Future."

I. PREPARE FOR THE FUTURE

First, prepare for the future by accepting Christ as your Saviour. Our Lord said, "He that believeth on me hath everlasting life" (John 6:47). It is hard to get people to see the simplicity of the Gospel, especially when their eyes are blinded by some religious dogma.

I spoke to a man a few hours ago who belonged to a certain church; and when I asked, "Are you saved?" he answered, "What do you mean?"

"Sir, are you a Christian?"

"What is a Christian?" Then he went on to tell me that he knew nothing of what I was talking about, that his entire hope was in church membership.

When I asked him to read one single verse from my Bible that supported his belief, he promptly told me that he knew nothing about the Word of God.

The first step of preparation for the future is to know Jesus Christ as Saviour. "He that hath the Son hath life; and he that hath not the Son of God hath not life" (I John 5:12).

In Christ we have the promise of eternal life.

We have the indwelling of the Holy Spirit. When we took Christ as Saviour, the Holy Spirit came in and took up His abode.

We have "the peace of God, which passeth all understanding." Jesus said to His disciples, "Peace I leave with you, my peace I give unto you: not as the world giveth, give I unto you. Let not your heart be troubled, neither let it be afraid" (John 14:27).

We don't have peace because of riches, pleasures, environment or gratification of the flesh. Peace comes by believing in Jesus Christ. We have peace because our sins are washed away. "But if we walk in the light, as he is in the light, we have fellowship one with another, and the blood of Jesus Christ his Son cleanseth us from all sin" (I John 1:7).

Second, we prepare for the future by obedience to His will. God has a will for your life! If you disobey Him, then there will come discord and disaster.

Young friend, if Christ has called you to a certain task, then obey. You have no right to wait even a single day or a single hour; at once say, "Yes, I will follow Him."

Parents, if God has spoken to you, then obey. You have no right to turn away from His plain command.

Husbands and wives, obey the Saviour, and the time to do it is today. Some people wait too long to do what God says.

The story was given by George Eliot of a very keen-minded lady. Her husband put secondary things first, neglected the chief things which make homelife gracious, beautiful, holy and blessed.

He rose early and toiled late and gave little attention, little consideration to his wife, until it was too late. He was set on getting property and more property and still more. One evening when he came home, his wife, Millie, was at death's door; and in a few hours she passed away.

That night the businessman was stirred out of his nightmare. The wife of his heart, the mother of his children, was now cold in death; he was dumbfounded and utterly overborne. Speechless was he in his overwhelming bereavement.

His wife's body was carried out to a quiet place; and after

the grave had been covered over with flowers and the people had gone, the husband threw himself across the grave and wailed out, "Millie! Millie! I did care for you! I loved you more than all else! Do you hear me now?"

She did not hear him.

This husband had failed in the same way that you fail if you put business first and do not do what God says.

Third, prepare for the future by turning from sin. I call your attention to two verses in Galatians 6:

"Be not deceived; God is not mocked: for whatsoever a man soweth, that shall he also reap.

"For he that soweth to his flesh shall of the flesh reap corruption; but he that soweth to the Spirit shall of the Spirit reap life everlasting."—Vss. 7,8.

Sin hurts today, but especially tomorrow. When sin is sown, there comes a reaping time. The future is colored by today. Sin will bring regret and sadness tomorrow.

Not only must we turn from sin, but we must help others to do so.

A preacher made it his business to talk to people about Christ whenever he could. One day he was attracted to a man who stood near him on a busy street. The man seemed to have a heavy heart. The preacher walked up and spoke to him, then took out a gospel tract and gave it to the man and asked if he were a Christian. He stated that he was not.

The stranger took the tract and looked at it. It was a small card picturing a high precipice overlooking a vast void across which was written the word *Eternity*. The man stood transfixed. "Thank you for handing me this," he said. "It must be a divine warning for me," and he told his story.

> I'm a drunkard. I have a fine family, a lovely wife and children. But I can't resist when these periodic cravings for liquor come over me. To save my family worry and disgrace, I came to this city, letting them think I would be away some days on business.

Actually, my plans called for getting liquor, a hotel room and drinking my fill.

I see it now. I was on the brink of the precipice and about to go over. I felt as though I was struck by some awful blow when I looked at this card. The word *death* and the word *eternity*—these are warnings.

Then the preacher told him about Christ, the Son of God. Then the man turned away from his sin and turned to the Saviour. The man said, "I'm going back home now to my wife and children, going back as one reclaimed from sin. Thank you for speaking to me."

Yes, one can prepare for the future by accepting Christ the Saviour. By obedience to His will and by turning from sin, we can prepare for the future.

II. DON'T FEAR THE FUTURE

We are speaking of the future as related to this life.

Moses gave the declarations of the book of Deuteronomy to the people of Israel. In Deuteronomy 33, he called the roll of the tribes, then he said the following:

"The eternal God is thy refuge, and underneath are the everlasting arms: and he shall thrust out the enemy from before thee; and shall say, Destroy them."—Vs. 27.

What was Moses saying? Simply this: "Don't fear the future."

Christ our Saviour tells us to fear not. These are simple verses that are very meaningful to the child of God:

"But seek ye first the kingdom of God, and his righteousness; and all these things shall be added unto you.

"Take therefore no thought for the morrow: for the morrow shall take thought for the things of itself. Sufficient unto the day is the evil thereof."—Matt. 6:33,34.

Paul asked in Romans 8:31, "If God be for us, who can be against us?" In verse 35 of that chapter he asks: "Who shall separate us from the love of Christ? shall tribulation, or distress, or persecution, or famine, or nakedness, or peril, or sword?"

Paul is saying not to fear.

He emphasizes the same truth in Philippians 4:

"Be careful for nothing; but in every thing by prayer and supplication with thanksgiving let your requests be made known unto God.

"And the peace of God, which passeth all understanding, shall keep your hearts and minds through Christ Jesus."—Vss. 6, 7.

In many places that loving apostle, John, told the people to have faith in God and not to fear. He said:

"There is no fear in love; but perfect love casteth out fear: because fear hath torment. He that feareth is not made perfect in love."—I John 4:18.

The Devil wants us to fear, but God wants us to fear not, for He is with us. We have His assurance, "I will never leave thee, nor forsake thee" (Heb. 13:5).

Fear not, for He opens doors for us. Paul said, "For a great door and effectual is opened unto me" (I Cor. 16:9).

Fear not, for He guides us. Jesus said about the Holy Spirit, "He will guide you into all truth" (John 16:13).

Fear not, for He gives success. It is my belief that God wants His children to be successful. The word *success* is found only one time in the Bible, in Joshua 1:8, but the theme of success is given throughout the Bible.

Fear is common to all. But we turn to our Lord and rest in Him, and there we find peace.

Love God, walk with God, and fear but one thing—being out of His will.

A young man felt the call of God to the ministry. During his university days, he was a strong intellect, was popular among his schoolmates, and had a personal magnetism that enabled him to achieve success in his field.

Though he felt a call of God to Christian work, the pull of the world was so strong that he deliberately turned away from the work God wanted him to do. He broke off his engagement to a Christian girl, who urged him to be loyal to the work of the ministry. He married a society leader whose family brought him social position and wealth.

He gained much from the world's standpoint, but oh, at what a cost! He lost interest in the church and in Christian work. His life was ruined. It showed in his unhappiness.

Someone has said:

> The greatest ruins of earth are not the Hanging Gardens of Babylon, nor the crumbling walls of the Parthenon at Athens, nor the Coliseum at Rome, but rather the ruins of a human soul that has yielded to the allurements of selfish interest.

III. REJOICE IN THE GLORIOUS PROSPECTS OF THE FUTURE

We have God's promises. The future is bright and exciting. Adoniram Judson said, "The future is as bright as the promises of God."

First, Christ is coming again. This is the brightest, happiest truth in the Bible for the child of God. With His coming, we have the resurrection, we have reunion, and we have rejoicing. With His coming, we are set free from the rotten sins of this world. With His coming, we're made free from the pressures of this life.

Second, we shall reign with Him. Paul said, "Do ye not know that the saints shall judge the world?" (I Cor. 6:2). We will have a place with our Saviour throughout eternity.

Third, the future means Heaven and all that the word implies. Jesus spoke about Hell thirteen times, but we have one beautiful picture of Heaven in John 14.

John, the apostle of love, spoke much about Hell, torment and suffering. But he also spoke about Heaven in Revelation 21 and 22.

The coming of our Lord is in the future.

Death is future. How near it is, we do not know. Death is all around us. One day we have the funeral for one of advanced years; another day we have the funeral for one just a few hours old. Every city has its cemetery. Every paper carries obituaries. The Bible says, "And as it is appointed unto men once to die, but after this the judgment" (Heb. 9:27).

The future holds Heaven for those who believe in Jesus Christ. The future holds Hell for those who die unsaved.

General Booth, founder and leader of the Salvation Army, said to some hundreds of his cadets when they were graduating from the training school:

> Young men, if I had my way, I would never have had you for years in this training home, but would have put you in Hell for twenty-four hours so that you could feel the pains and pangs of the damned; that you could hear their weeping, wailing and gnashing of teeth; and that you could see their torments.
>
> I would have then let you out to go into the world to warn men and women to flee from the wrath to come. And I would be sure of this: you would never take the work easy or treat it negligently while you were in it.

General Booth was entirely right. If we could get people to see the awfulness of Hell, it would solve many problems in our soul winning and witnessing.

But perhaps we should turn the story to the other side. Perhaps we should say to Christians, "If you had just twenty-four hours in Heaven, then you would come back better able to persuade men to turn from sin, the filth, the trash of this world and turn to Jesus Christ, the Son of God."

But wait a minute. I have news for you. One of these days I shall be in the presence of my Lord and enjoying all the bliss of Heaven, but right now I have a little bit of heaven on earth. I have Christ as my Saviour and the joy of the Lord in my heart.

The Christian and the future! There is just a heartbeat between you and eternity. For the saved, there is just a heartbeat between you and Heaven. For the lost, there is just a heartbeat between you and Hell. I beseech you who are unsaved to turn to the Lord Jesus Christ now and receive Him as your Saviour, so you can enjoy Heaven with all Christians.

IT'S LATER THAN YOU THINK

"Boast not thyself of to morrow; for thou knowest not what a day may bring forth."—Prov. 27:1.

"Whereas ye know not what shall be on the morrow. For what is your life? It is even a vapour, that appeareth for a little time, and then vanisheth away.

"For that ye ought to say, If the Lord will, we shall live, and do this, or that."—Jas. 4:14,15.

Some years ago while in St. Petersburg, Florida for special meetings, I bought the morning newspaper. The headline was "166 Die in Jet Crash." A Mexicana Airlines plane out of Mexico City had crashed into a mountain on its way to California. There were no survivors. Death came suddenly. Earthly life was over for the crew and passengers. All were thrown into eternity in a moment's time. Leaving Mexico City they had expected to have an enjoyable trip to cities in the United States, but they never reached their destination. "Boast not thyself of to morrow; for thou knowest not what a day may bring forth."

This may be my last meeting. This could be your last service. What we do, we had better do now. It is always later than we think! "Lord, I want to do Your will every day"—this prayer will have a bearing on tomorrow, the next day, and the next, and days out ahead.

On April 1 the same city, I met with Dr. Dale Crowley of Washington, D.C., whom I had known for many years. He edited a paper *The Capital Voice*. He placed in my hands a copy of the last issue. On the front page was an article by Dr. Crowley, "It's Later Than You Think." I want to give you the story.

A widower in Quebec, Canada, died and left a small legacy to his daughters. A few days after the funeral, the daughters sat down to discuss their future and what they would do. The younger one, Louise, said, "I would like to travel and see some of the places we have read about."

But Miriam said, "We don't have enough money to do that." So they didn't go.

They bought a small country store, stocked it, and the people came. Soon it became a successful business.

One day after some Florida customers had left the store, Louise said, "Why don't we close down the business for the winter and go down to Florida where it is warm?"

But Miriam said, "We can't do that. The people would start trading somewhere else."

A few years went by. The sisters had earned enough money in the store to last for the rest of their lives. Again Louise said, "Let's sell out now. Let's take a trip to California, then on to Mexico City and to other places south."

But again the older sister, Miriam, said, "Nobody would give us what the business is worth. Let's hold onto it."

So, they kept on working, Miriam never consenting to a trip, and Louise always wanting to go somewhere.

One night in January, Louise set out alone from the store to her home. Taking a shortcut through the field, she slipped and fell, fracturing her hip. No one heard her cry for help. When the neighbor found her the next morning, pneumonia had set it.

In three days Louise was dead. The funeral service,

they say, was one of the most elaborate ever conducted in that part of the country.

Miriam bought and had sent in a magnificent bronze coffin. Later she put on the grave a carved tombstone, shipped all the way from Vermont, marking the final resting-place of her sister.

But in the spring Miriam made a strange request of the authorities: "I would like to move Louise's body to California." They gave her permission.

The body in the casket was placed on the plane. Miriam went along. She buried Louise in California.

A few months later she obtained another disinterment permit, this time to take the coffin to Mexico City. She accompanied the body. There she had her sister buried.

The last report was, the bronze coffin had been shipped out of Mexico City to Havana.

The story has a meaning. The sister who had not wanted to use her and her sister's money for travel, to appease her own conscience, moved the body from place to place.

Dr. Crowley commented that doubtless even now a dear old lady was sitting on the front porch of some hotel with a body ready to be placed in a grave in that city, moving it from place to place.

A lesson comes out of that story. We keep putting things off. Miriam put it off and kept saying, "Later, later." But they never did get to do what Louise wanted to do.

We are the same way. We keep putting things off and saying we will do thus and so at a later time, but we never do it! We are always hoping to do something big for God, but we never do it! We are always planning to pray more, read our Bible through, but we never get around to it. We are always planning to win souls, but we never do.

I repeat my text: "Boast not thyself of to morrow, for thou knowest not what a day may bring forth....For what is your life? It is even a vapour, that appeareth for a little time, and then vanisheth away."

What is the time for all of us? I suggest some things.

I. IT IS THE TIME FOR GOD'S PEOPLE TO LEARN THE SECRET OF VICTORIOUS LIVING

All around us are defeated Christians, who are like little pups that have been whipped with a stick. Christians are discouraged and disgruntled. They go about complaining and murmuring. Churches are not getting people in. Mission programs are failing. Sunday schools are dying in many places. Prayer meetings are languishing. And soul winning never happens.

What is the meaning of victorious living? Giving up sin. Whatever it may be, turn from it. Hate sin. When Satan is in control, standards are lowered. Holy ambitions are cast aside. Sin has power to weaken and destroy. People don't hate sin.

Victorious living means dying to self and being filled with the Holy Spirit. I mentioned already that Paul said, "I die daily." Jesus said, "Except a corn of wheat fall into the ground and die, it abideth alone: but if it die, it bringeth forth much fruit." Do you know the secret of dying to self? When did you die?

There is a little book entitled *How to Die Daily*. This is so important. For victorious living, one must empty self of sin and be willing for God to control his life.

Again, victorious living means accepting God's will.

I shall never forget that Sunday morning in the old country church outside of Louisville, at Cedar Creek. When the minister preached, this eighteen-year-old sat way back in the corner with a bunch of high school boys. When he said, "I believe God is calling someone to preach the Gospel," I felt that he had spoken to me.

I left my seat and walked to the front. I said to my pastor, "I believe God wants me to preach." Of course, I wasn't sure what it would be, what type of ministry I would have. The pastor had me stand in the front of the church. He said, "Maybe there are other young men who feel the same way." Eight others came and stood by me—nine of us there in front of the church. But I am the only one who ever preached. The others turned back.

One man, W. A. Lucky, came by, shook my hand, bent over and whispered in my ear, "Young man, if God has called you, dare do nothing else." Then he said, "When I was your age, God called me, but I turned away from that call to make money, and I have never been happy." Then he said this: "I pray every day, but I have never prayed without being conscious of being out of the will of God."

Wouldn't it be awful to feel that way?

I am the only one out of the nine to preach, and only one other is living today, as far as I know, and he is in a cell in the federal penitentiary in Atlanta, Georgia, and over seventy-five years of age. All the others are gone. One boy who had stood by my side was named Emmons. Just past his thirtieth birthday, he went down back of his house, put a rifle to his head and killed himself. The other young men never accomplished anything. Maybe God did not call them—I don't know. Maybe He did call them, and they did not heed the call.

Victorious living means accepting God's will and doing it. God has a will for everyone. He is your Father and will help you. He will help you carry your burdens and be victorious.

In the will of God, you will shine for Christ. In the will of God, you can rejoice even when the body is weak. In the will of God, you can overcome temptations.

Now, for over fifty years of ministry, I have enjoyed seeking daily to do what I felt God wanted me to do. I have failed many times, but I want to do His will.

So, it is time for victorious living, not defeated living.

II. IT IS TIME FOR GOD'S PEOPLE
TO PRAY FOR REVIVAL
IN OUR CHURCHES

It is time for God's people to pray, yes, to agonize, for revival. Many churches are failing. They are cold. They are following a liberal theology. They, though living, are dead.

We need revival, an old-fashioned revival, with plain preaching on repentance and calling people to be separated from the world; a return to the old-fashioned soul-winning methods of going after people and witnessing to them.

An agonizing for revival—an old-fashioned, heart-searching, moving revival upon our hearts—is what God wants. And He is ready to give it when we meet His conditions.

Indiana is my home state. I was born in southern Indiana amidst the hills and hollows, where it is rough going; but in the middle of the state are beautiful farmlands.

I was preaching in an Indiana city. The next morning a fine Christian man, a medical doctor, took me to the airport. He had an outstanding testimony for Christ.

I had heard that around Indianapolis, on those big, beautiful farms, farmers were having financial trouble. They had bought expensive equipment, then could not pay for it, so they were selling out.

This doctor and I discussed the matter. He told me that one man bought a farm and expensive equipment, some costing as much as one hundred thousand dollars for just one piece. Then some farmers began to fail, so they were going out of business, selling equipment and giving up.

This man failed along with the rest of them. He sold everything and paid off every debt on his farm. Then he said, "I'm going to start again. But this time I will try it the old-fashioned way."

So he bought some horses, mules, old-fashioned plows,

mowing machines, and so forth, and employed some of the farmers who had lost their farms. The doctor said this man is making a living and, in fact, making money by doing it the old-fashioned way! Also he was helping others make a good living.

I am not saying we have to do like that, but we need to use Bible methods—the simple methods that have always worked throughout centuries and will work now if we use them.

Today a church is considered pretty much of a flop if it doesn't have a TV program. The idea is, you need a TV program to raise money. Or you have to have a radio network to make it, or a paper with advertising. I am not against some things when they are done right; but we have an idea that modern advertising, social events, lowering standards, and swanky preachers who please the ears of the people will bring us what we need.

What we need is the power of God, the Holy Spirit's power upon us, to move us, to shake us and to bring us to the place where God can give revival. We need revival for the individual heart. The individual must be touched.

Here is an expensive grand piano that costs many thousands of dollars. Let there be one discordant note, and see what happens. Take out middle C, and see what happens. Let it be out of tune, and see what happens. Let G above middle C be out of tune, and see what happens.

I am trying to emphasize that your idea of revival needs to be personal. You need to say, "Dear Lord, revive me! I need revival. I need the stirring of my heart. I want to be right with God."

Revival means confession. "If we confess our sins, he is faithful and just to forgive us our sins, and to cleanse us from all unrighteousness."

Revival means dedication. "I beseech you therefore,

brethren, by the mercies of God, that ye present your bodies a living sacrifice" (Rom. 12:1)—everything on the altar, everything surrendered to Him, no holding back, but saying, "Lord, take it all, everything!"

In the book *Back to Bethel*, F. B. Meyer tells how the Lord dealt with him. Though a minister, his life had been unsettled for some time. He invited a young minister to speak in his church. This minister led Meyer to believe he possessed a secret which Meyer did not have. He went home that night determined to settle the matter and make a full surrender to Christ.

Read what Meyer said:

> It seemed as though Jesus was by my side and as if I took from my pocket a large bunch of keys and took from that bunch one tiny key, then held up to Jesus the bunch with the one missing and said to Him, "Here are the keys of my life."
>
> He looked at me sadly and asked, "Are all there?"
>
> I answered, "All but one tiny one to a small cupboard. It is so small that it cannot amount to anything."
>
> Christ replied, "Child, if you cannot trust Me with everything, you cannot trust Me with anything."
>
> At last I said, "Lord, I cannot give the key, but I am willing to have You come and take it."
>
> It seemed He came and opened my fingers and took the key, then went straight to that cupboard, unlocked it, and saw there a thing that was unacceptable. He said, "This must go. You must never go this way again."
>
> The moment He took the thing from me, He took the desire away, and I began to hate it. Then I yielded myself absolutely to Him and said, "From this night, I want Thee to do as Thou wilt with my life."

Friend, have you some hidden cupboard where you are harboring a thing that is killing your joy? Before you can have God's best, you must let Him show what the unclean thing is which has choked your spiritual vitality. There must be a surrender of everything—your time, your talents, your money, your home, your family and anything which would displease your God.

Revival means restoration, making things right, returning to the fundamentals of prayer, church attendance, tithing, and such like.

Revival means a return to holy living.

Revival means laughter *and* tears. Am I right? We have gotten to a place in much of our religious life and in our churches where we are somewhat straight in our ways, and we feel like anything away from that is not going to work. There are no tears shed, no rejoicing in the Lord. Great revivals will be accompanied by tears *and* joy.

Revival means conviction. We have lost our convictions about sin, about righteousness, about winning the lost and about the local church.

Revival means compassion for souls and seeking to bring people to the Saviour. When Jesus saw the multitudes, He was moved with compassion because they fainted and were scattered abroad as sheep having no shepherd. Jesus, the compassionate One!

Praise God, we are here tonight because He loved us so much that He gave His Son to die on the cross. That is compassion.

Revival means caring for souls, weeping over sinners, a hunger to see God move.

It is time for God's people to pray for revival and let that revival start with you. Keep in mind that you are important. You are just one in this church, but you are important. If you are not right, the thing may fail.

22

THE LAST CHAPTER IN A GREAT STORY

"And he said, My presence shall go with thee, and I will give thee rest."—Exod. 33:14.

The story of Moses is a simple one. For forty years he played, prepared and performed. The story of Moses in the last third of his life is explained in our text. God said, "My presence shall go with thee, and I will give thee rest."

Here is a word for our youth: "My presence shall go with thee." The eternal God will not prevent the storms, but He will be with you in the storms.

Here is a word for the troubled: "My presence shall go with thee." In times of stress and uncertainty, we had better know that we have His presence with us.

Here is a word for leaders, as Moses was: "My presence shall go with thee." The Lord is saying to leaders, "Don't put your faith in the sinking sands of time but in the steadfast Rock of Ages."

"My *presence* shall go with thee." This means sincere prayer, true worship, obedience to God, biblical preaching and compassion never fail.

"My presence shall go with thee." He will be with us in *all* the chapters of life—in the first chapter and in the last chapter.

He gives guidance, strength and peace. He gives power. He gives fellowship.

His presence takes away fear about today and tomorrow, fear about problems, both financial and physical.

His presence takes away doubts. Yesterday I saw a letter sent to me by a missionary, who is having doubts about the Bible. He is asking questions about the veracity of the Word. He sent a full page of questions. The Devil has upset his thinking.

God's presence takes away weakness. Physical weakness and mental distress come from within.

As we come to this last Sunday of the month in this house of worship, I think of the years of victories and defeats. I think of the beautiful days as well as the ugly ones.

My mind goes back to Moses, the leader of Israel, the mightiest of men. God said to him, "My presence shall go with thee, and I will give thee rest." I then turned to Deuteronomy and considered chapters 31, 32, 33 and 34. Moses was 120 years old. He said, "I can no more go out and come in" (31:2). Yet when he died, "His eye was not dim, nor his natural force abated" (34:7).

I. THE PAST REVIEWED

Deuteronomy is a book of review. Moses reminded the people again of all that God had done for them. They were ready to cross over into Canaan. He reviewed the goodness of God and the victories they had won through faith in God.

Moses did not review blindly. He told the good and the bad. He called upon the people, "Beware lest thou forget the LORD, which brought thee forth out of the land of Egypt, from the house of bondage" (Deut. 6:12).

We must remember the goodness of God to us. In this building many thousands have heard the preaching of God's

Word. We have had hundreds of blessed hours of worship. We have seen thousands repent and believe in Christ. We have watched thousands obey Christ in the waters of baptism. We have seen thousands come to the front for rededication. We have seen hundreds give themselves to the service of Christ to be pastors, missionaries or Christian workers.

In the past, we have received enough offerings to send the Gospel to every part of the world. Millions of dollars have been given to the cause of Christ at home and abroad: 496 missionaries, 71 chapels, Union Gospel Mission, Camp Joy.

For thirty-four years in this edifice, we have preached and sung the Gospel: in regular services, revival services, missionary conferences, Bible conferences.

As we review the past, we would not be honest if we did not face our failures and mistakes. Sometimes we have failed to remember God's promises. Like Israel, we walked in unbelief. We trusted in self.

Sometimes we failed to respond to God's chastening hand. He reached down to correct us, but we were insensitive to His touch. Sometimes we failed to obey our Lord in witnessing. Sometimes we failed to give our youth and our money for missions. Sometimes we behaved in ways contrary to our Lord's desire. Sometimes we lost faith. We doubted God.

Moses had his problems too. We have had ours. Only the grace of God kept us going.

II. THE PRESENT ENJOYED

God is ever the same—in Moses' day and in this day. Moses enjoyed the present blessings of God. God wants us to enjoy our present blessings! We are saved by grace, we are secure in Him, and we can have His peace. Today we are kept by His hand; today we can pray and feel His presence;

today we can rest in Him, our Intercessor; today we know
He is preparing a place for us.

III. THE FUTURE ANTICIPATED

Moses looked ahead. He went up to the top of Mount
Pisgah over against Jericho, "and the LORD shewed him all
the land" given to Israel.

Remember, Moses was in good health—120 years old but
still a strong man. He had spiritual sight. He could look
ahead and see the battles, the victories, the defeats. Moses
was submissive. When the Lord refused him permission to
enter the land of promise, he didn't complain.

Here was the last chapter of a great life, but there was
more to come. Hundreds of years later, Moses came down
and talked to the Lord Jesus. "And, behold, there talked
with him [the Lord] two men, which were Moses and Elias"
(Luke 9:30).

The last chapter should remind us of sin's treachery
and danger.

Israel failed. Even Moses failed. We too fail! We forget
how awful sin is. We forget that it cheats us out of God's
full blessings.

Only yesterday a man cried to me about his failures and
what they had cost him.

Yes, the last chapter often brings regrets. The last chapter should give us pleasant memories of God's goodness.

Moses looked back, and when he saw the goodness of
God, he was thankful. We too look back and remember—
remember our salvation, remember the answers to prayer,
remember the guidance of God.

The last chapter should leave us looking to the future.
The last chapter is not the end. There is a Heaven, a Hell,
and both are eternal.

Look ahead; the best is yet to come! Christ is coming. We shall be in His presence. We shall reign with our Lord on this earth.

"And so shall we ever be with the Lord."—I Thess. 4:17.

"FRUIT IN OLD AGE"

Dr. Roberson's approximate preaching itinerary since he
retired from pastorate of Highland Park
Baptist Church, April 27, 1983

1983 (After April 27)
Athens, GA
Rosemount, MN
Fayetteville, NC
Jacksonville, FL
Kennesaw, GA
Baton Rouge, LA
Garland, TX
Washington, GA
Brunswick, GA
Murfreesboro, TN
Powell, TN
Huntsville, AL
Alexander City, AL
Chattanooga, TN
Dalton, GA
Cincinnati, OH
South Pittsburgh, TN
Murfreesboro, TN
Oliver Springs, TN
Morristown, TN
Stevenson, AL
Kansas City, MO
Greenville, NC
St. Paul, MN
Gallatin, TN
McLeansville, NC
Landrum, SC
Sanford, NC
College Park, GA
Sevierville, TN
Auburn, IN
Pigeon Forge, TN
Baltimore, MD
Doraville, GA

Dayton, TN
Decatur, GA
Greenville, MS
Dunlap, TN
Macon, GA
Hartselle, AL
Athens, TN
Orange Park, FL
Bangor, ME
Douglasville, GA
Charlotte, NC
Hindman, KY
Dalton, GA
Prattville, AL
Blountville, TN
Cincinnati, OH
Garland, TX
Fayetteville, NC
Raleigh, NC
Morrow, GA
Chatsworth, GA
Louisville, KY
Kingsport, TN
Bensalem, PA
Kokomo, IN
Tucker, GA
Grass Lake, MI
Walkertown, NC
Jefferson City, TN
Bear, DE
Louisville, KY
Ephrata, PA
Stone Mountain, GA
Knoxville, TN
Sevierville, TN

Springfield, TN
Blountville, TN
Statesville, NC
Prichard, AL
Ft. Worth, TX
Madison, TN
Louisville, KY

1984
Gadsden, AL
Hodgenville, KY
Decatur, GA
Burbank, IL
Hollywood, FL
Manchester, TN
West Columbia, SC
Murfreesboro, TN
Ashville, AL
Garland, TX
Williamsport, PA
Bridgeport, AL
Forest Park, GA
Orlando, FL
Hendersonville, TN
Atlanta, GA
Longview, TX
Columbus, GA
Cedartown, GA
LaFayette, GA
Memphis, TN
Wetumpka, AL
Chicago, IL
Milford, OH
Ft. Pierce, FL
Raleigh, NC

Baton Rouge, LA
Crossville, TN
Plainfield, IN
Riverview, FL
Douglasville, GA
Delray Beach, FL
Somerset, KY
Dalton, GA
Hammond, IN
Macon, GA
Montpelier, OH
Lakeland, FL
Canton, OH
Omaha, NE
Warm Springs, GA
Rosemount, MN
Westminster, MD
Princeton, WV
Eden Prairie, MN
Festus, MO
Cullman, AL
Jacksonville, NC
Englewood, FL
Mannington, WV
Grove City, OH
Covington, IN
Independence, MO
Raleigh, NC
Statesboro, GA
Owensboro, KY
Gainesville, GA
Portsmouth, OH
Lynchburg, VA
St. Albans, WV
White Plains, MD
Bowling Green, KY
Proctorville, OH
Dalton, GA
Tyler, TX
Garland, TX
Monticello, FL
Corpus Christi, TX
Oakland, CA

Blountsville, AL
Smyrna, TN
Madison, TN
Dundee, FL
Charleston, WV
Little Rock, AR
Detroit, MI
Chattanooga, TN
Franklin, IN
Bristol, TN
Ringgold, GA
Stone Mountain, GA
Baton Rouge, LA
Sanford, NC
Oak Forest, IL
Schererville, IN
Radcliff, KY
Garland, TX
Murfreesboro, TN
Morrow, GA
Gaithersburg, MD
Shelbyville, TN
Jacksonville, FL
Lebanon, IN
Murfreesboro, TN
Gadsden, AL
Pinellas Park, FL
Atlanta, GA
Spokane, WA
Lenoir City, TN
Chambersburg, PA
Jackson, TN
Gretna, LA
Meridian, MS
Lakeland, FL
Powell, TN
Hattiesburg, MS
Gallipolis, OH
Cedartown, GA
Panama City, FL
Cleveland, OH
Lewisville, TX
Orange Park, FL

Chattanooga, TN
Memphis, TN
Gray, LA
Kingsport, TN
Morrow, GA
Kennesaw, GA
Amsterdam, NY
Cleveland, TN
Lima, OH
Birmingham, AL
Bridgeport, AL
Glasgow, KY
Chickamauga, GA
Oxford, AL
Gadsden, AL
Chattanooga, TN

1985
Crossville, TN
Chattanooga, TN
Oswego, IL
Rossville, GA
Benton, TN
New Port Richey, FL
Manchester, TN
Fredericksburg, VA
Tucker, GA
Houston, TX
Cuernavaca, Mexico
Chesapeake, VA
Crown Point, IN
Chatsworth, GA
Raleigh, NC
New Castle, DE
Knoxville, TN
Louisville, KY
Conyers, GA
Milford, OH
Gadsden, AL
Pelham, AL
Garland, TX
Indianapolis, IN
Little Hocking, OH

Jacksonville, FL
Aurora, IL
Lawrenceburg, KY
Madison, TN
Chattanooga, TN
Festus, MO
Columbia, MD
Stuart, FL
Brockton, MA
Linwood, PA
Gadsden, AL
Morrisonville, IL
Springville, AL
Oliver Springs, TN
Blountville, TN
Scottsboro, AL
Oxford, AL
Rincon, GA
Memphis, TN
Covington, IN
Athens, TN
Guin, AL
Westminster, MD
Mt. Airy, NC
Washington, IL
Tyler, TX
Bessemer, AL
Evensville, TN
Aiken, SC
Brooklyn, NY
Bensalem, PA
Greenville, SC
Madison, VA
Chattanooga, TN
Sellersville, PA
Easley, SC
Middletown, OH
Meridian, MS
Chickamauga, GA
Virginia Beach, VA
Salem, VA
Panama City, FL
Sylacauga, AL

Rossville, GA
Sequatchie, TN
Young Harris, GA
Gardendale, AL
Upper Marlboro, MD
Tampa, FL
Chattanooga, TN
Gainesville, GA
Belton, SC
Birmingham, AL
Forest Park, GA
Flat Rock, AL
Memphis, TN
Yukon, OK
Oklahoma City, OK
Decatur, GA
Midland, TX
West Columbia, SC
Graniteville, SC
Hartselle, AL
Madisonville, KY
Suwanee, GA
McDonald, TN
Kinston, NC
Montpelier, OH
Madison, AL
Laurens, SC
Shelbyville, TN
Villa Rica, GA
Jackson, TN
Marietta, GA
Richmond, VA
Hopewell, VA
Greensboro, NC
Northglenn, CO
Mansfield, OH
Acworth, GA
Lilburn, GA
Connersville, IN
Danville, IL
Chattanooga, TN
Shreveport, LA
Tullahoma, TN

Greenville, MS
South Point, OH
Valdosta, GA
Hickory, NC
South St. Paul, MN
Rand, WV
Gibsonton, FL
Wallingford, CT
Soddy Daisy, TN
Bradenton, FL
Mocksville, NC
Valdosta, GA
Cahokia, IL
Newington, CT
Fayetteville, NC
Mannington, WV
Columbiana, OH
Jacksonville, FL
Crawfordsville, IN
5 Islands of West Indies
Oxford, AL
Boston, MA
Gadsden, AL
Atlanta, GA

1986
Atlanta, GA
Harrison, TN
Rome, GA
Kermit, TX
Chatsworth, GA
Chattanooga, TN
Canton, GA
Jefferson, GA
Roswell, GA
Manchester, TN
Birmingham, AL
Forest Park, GA
Nashville, TN
Houston, TX
Cuernavaca, Mexico
Waycross, GA
Tallapoosa, GA

Norcross, GA
De Soto, TX
Baton Rouge, LA
LaFayette, GA
Walkertown, NC
Trenton, GA
Tabb, VA
Rossville, GA
Festus, MO
Sayre, PA
Decatur, AL
Garland, TX
Danville, IL
Durham, NC
Terre Haute, IN
New Smyrna Beach, FL
Palmer, TN
Chattanooga, TN
Crown Point, IN
Pinellas Park, FL
Morrow, GA
Milford, OH
Arlington, TX
Charlotte, NC
Goldsboro, NC
Powell, TN
Belleville, MI
Grand Haven, MI
Rossville, GA
Indianapolis, IN
New London, OH
Tyler, TX
Mt. Pleasant, TX
Fayetteville, GA
Soddy Daisy, TN
Portsmouth, VA
Huntsville, AL
Kentwood, MI
Columbia, MD
Bath, SC
Rossville, GA
Lexington, NC
Lakeland, FL

Heber Springs, AR
Chattanooga, TN
Huntsville, AL
Richmond, VA
Greenville, SC
Cartersville, GA
Bolingbrook, IL
Winder, GA
Indianapolis, IN
Atkinson, NH
Southington, CT
Shreveport, LA
Florala, AL
Paterson, NJ
Jamestown, TN
Thomasville, GA
Apache Creek, NM
Mt. Pleasant, PA
Scottsboro, AL
Murfreesboro, TN
Ocoee, FL
Graysville, TN
White Sulphur Springs,
  WV
Loganville, GA
Waco, TX
Black River Falls, WI
Chattanooga, TN
Calhoun, GA
Garland, TX
San Antonio, TX
Los Angeles, CA
Salisbury, NC
Birmingham, AL
Chattanooga, TN
Waco, TX
Vienna, GA
Mocksville, NC
Cincinnati, OH
Hot Springs, AR
Santa Clara, CA
Villa Rica, GA
Molino, FL

Murfreesboro, TN
Little Hocking, OH
Stone Mountain, GA
Curwensville, PA
Raleigh, NC
Graniteville, SC
Webster, FL
Chattanooga, TN
Decatur, AL
Washington, IL
Norfolk, VA
Upper Marlboro, MD
Mobile, AL
Bradenton, FL
Springfield, TN
Ocala, FL
Greenville, MI
Soddy Daisy, TN
South St. Paul, MN
Odenton, MD
Chattanooga, TN
Ft. Worth, TX
Chesapeake, VA
Hanson, MA
Selmer, TN
Tucker, GA
Ft. Worth, TX
Huntingburg, IN
Tupelo, MS
Thomasville, GA
Rising Fawn, GA
Franklin, IN
Birmingham, AL
Des Moines, IA
Summerville, GA
Harrison, TN
Gadsden, AL
Mission, TX
Graysville, TN
Rossville, GA

1987
Huntsville, AL

Decatur, GA
Villa Rica, GA
Morris, OK
Manchester, TN
Trenton, GA
Warren, MI
Canton, GA
Lyons, GA
Cuernavaca, Mexico
Morrow, GA
Tucker, GA
North Ft. Myers, FL
Monteagle, TN
Chesapeake, VA
New Castle, DE
Conyers, GA
Cowan, TN
Newport News, VA
Floral City, FL
Lakeside Park, KY
Grand Rapids, MI
Brooklyn, NY
Durham, NC
Dalton, GA
Burlington, NC
Knoxville, TN
Winder, GA
Pensacola, FL
Montgomery, AL
Ravenswood, WV
Reynoldsburg, OH
Morrow, GA
Panama City, FL
Pinellas Park, FL
Panama City, FL
Milford, OH
Gulfport, MS
Oklahoma City, OK
Rossville, GA
Asheboro, NC
Ripley, WV
Chattanooga, TN
Madison, TN

Guin, AL
Morristown, TN
Ft. Worth, TX
Longview, TX
San Antonio, TX
Sevierville, TN
Chattanooga, TN
Florence, AL
Albany, GA
Orlando, FL
Lilburn, GA
Chattanooga, TN
Warrenton, VA
Massillon, OH
Mansfield, OH
Lexington, NC
Dothan, AL
Great Falls, MT
Seymour, IA
Blairsville, GA
Harrison, TN
Rossville, GA
Sandusky, OH
Corpus Christi, TX
Apache Creek, NM
Farmington, NM
Albuquerque, NM
Rock Hill, SC
Signal Mountain, TN
Homasassa Springs, FL
Hartselle, AL
Bainbridge, GA
Morrow, GA
Red Bank, TN
Bay Shore, NY
Avenel, NJ
Canton, OH
Peoria, IL
Los Angeles, CA
Douglasville, GA
Columbus, GA
Oklahoma City, OK
Decatur, IL

Downers Grove, IL
Chesapeake, VA
Radcliff, KY
Roscoe, IL
Kings Mills, OH
Angola, IN
Muncy, PA
Waycross, GA
Dunn, NC
Mocksville, NC
Andalusia, IL
Chattanooga, TN
Spokane, WA
South San Diego, CA
Dallas, TX
Clinton, MD
Ft. Worth, TX
Savannah, OH
Marietta, OH
Winter Haven, FL
Chattanooga, TN
Columbia, MD
Mogadore, OH
Birmingham, AL
Shreveport, LA
Jacksonville, FL
Green Valley, AZ
Soddy Daisy, TN
St. Amant, LA
East Ridge, TN
Decatur, AL
Bessemer, AL
Rossville, GA
Festus, MO
Harrison, TN
Gadsden, AL
Scottsboro, AL
Chattanooga, TN
Chickamauga, GA
Cedar Lake, IN
Jasper, TN

1988
Columbus, GA
Owensboro, KY
Pellston, MI
Morris, OK
Manchester, TN
Lake City, GA
Montgomery, AL
Birmingham, AL
Acworth, GA
Silver Springs, FL
Americus, GA
Tampa, FL
Orange Park, FL
Palatka, FL
Riverview, FL
North Ft. Myers, FL
Valdosta, GA
Jasper, AL
Bradyville, TN
Newport News, VA
Oliver Springs, TN
Albany, GA
Mansfield, OH
Miami, FL
Huntsville, AL
Mobile, AL
Ocala, FL
Des Moines, IA
South St. Paul, MN
Wintersville, OH
Lewisville, TX
Chattanooga, TN
Milford, OH
Pontiac, MI
Clintwood, VA
Knoxville, TN
Louisville, KY
Pensacola, FL
Clinton, MD
Morrow, GA
Indiana, PA
Terre Haute, IN

Pinellas Park, FL
Walkertown, NC
Buford, GA
Kingston, TN
Chattanooga, TN
Lanett, AL
Jacksonville, FL
Oxford, AL
Chattanooga, TN
Ringgold, GA
Lakeland, FL
San Leandro, CA
Sevierville, TN
Los Angeles, CA
Meridian, MS
Pilot Mountain, NC
Canton, GA
Chattanooga, TN
Morganton, NC
Antioch, TN
Hooker, GA
Florala, AL
Dalton, GA
Cahokia, IL
Red Bank, TN
Middletown, OH
Mocksville, NC
Salisbury, NC
Jeremiah, KY
Rossville, GA
Hindman, KY
Greenville, SC
LaFollette, TN
Charleston, WV
Ephrata, PA
Paterson, NJ
Birmingham, AL
Hueytown, AL
Chattanooga, TN
New Bloomfield, PA
Trenton, GA
Dayton, OH
Calhoun, GA

Douglasville, GA
Marshall, TX
Morris, OK
Oklahoma City, OK
Hanover, PA
North Salem, IN
Selmer, TN
Warner Robins, GA
Carroll, OH
Burlington, NC
Atlanta, GA
Cleveland, TN
Lawrenceville, GA
Matthews, NC
Northfield, MA
Warrenton, VA
Garland, TX
Englewood, FL
Bristol, VA
Whites Creek, TN
Angola, IN
Belpre, OH
Cowan, TN
Murfreesboro, TN
Richmond, VA
Loganville, GA
Elkview, WV
Gallipolis Ferry, WV
Murfreesboro, TN
Middletown, OH
Chattanooga, TN
Orlando, FL
Philadelphia, PA
Salisbury, NC
Lithia Springs, GA
Little Hocking, OH
Stockton, CA
Waco, TX
Soddy Daisy, TN
Crown Point, IN
Belleville, IL
Chattanooga, TN
Carlsbad, NM

Clayton, NC
Harrison, TN
Rossville, GA
Benton, TN
Nashville, TN
Harrison, TN

1989
Chattanooga, TN
Belton, SC
Colbert, GA
Westminster, MD
Duluth, GA
Manchester, TN
Lilburn, GA
Morrow, GA
Martinsville, IN
Louisville, KY
Ripley, WV
Bowling Green, KY
Bristol, TN
Decatur, AL
Tempe, AZ
Fairfax, VA
Tallahassee, FL
Butler, PA
Independence, MO
Blountville, TN
Hartselle, AL
Graniteville, SC
Louisville, KY
Athens, AL
Connersville, IN
Sellersville, PA
Newport, TN
Ona, WV
Huntington, WV
Charlotte, NC
Chattanooga, TN
Pensacola, FL
Birchwood, TN
Inver Grove Heights,
   MN

Hattiesburg, MS
Athens, TN
Hixson, TN
Whitwell, TN
Crown Point, IN
Griffin, GA
Morgantown, IN
English, IN
Birmingham, AL
Lynchburg, VA
McNeill, MS
Chattanooga, TN
Athens, TN
Douglasville, GA
Anderson, SC
Ballard, WV
Norcross, GA
Greenville, SC
Dayton, OH
Lexington, NC
Pikeville, TN
Gallipolis, OH
Belpre, OH
Lima, OH
Newark, CA
Fremont, CA
Santa Clara, CA
Middletown, OH
Miami, FL
Rossville, GA
Murfreesboro, TN
Hueytown, AL
Chatsworth, GA
Greenville, SC
Findlay, OH
Randleman, NC
Shelby, NC
Richmond, VA
Quincy, MI
Richmond, VA
Greeneville, TN
Winston-Salem, NC
Pilot Mountain, NC

Trenton, GA
Fairfield, AL
Memphis, TN
Madisonville, KY
Williamstown, VA
Vassar, MI
Blue Ridge, VA
Harrison, TN
Garland, TX
Rossville, GA
Morrow, GA
Greeneville, TN
Murfreesboro, TN
Chattanooga, TN
Lexington, KY
Milford, OH
Stanfield, NC
Adrian, MI
Poland, OH
Ringgold, GA
Springfield, TN
LaFollette, TN
Delray Beach, FL
West Columbia, SC
Powell, TN
Winder, GA
Resaca, GA
Columbus, GA
Crossville, TN
Jupiter, FL
St. Petersburg, FL
Soddy Daisy, TN
Crown Point, IN
Chattanooga, TN
Chattanooga, TN

1990
Chattanooga, TN
Harned, KY
Toast, NC
Manchester, TN
Tunnel Hill, GA
Gatlinburg, TN

Cartersville, GA
Kansas City, MO
Lake City, GA
Riverdale, GA
Bowling Green, KY
Oklahoma City, OK
Ft. Myers, FL
Americus, GA
Chattanooga, TN
Jacksonville, FL
Nitro, WV
Columbiana, OH
Palmyra, TN
Hixson, TN
Westminster, MD
De Soto, TX
South Elgin, IL
Houston, TX
Montgomery, AL
Carbon Hill, AL
Tampa, FL
Lake City, GA
Louisville, KY
Festus, MO
Sedalia, MO
Chattanooga, TN
Bear, DE
Southington, CT
Athens, TN
Morrow, GA
Logansport, IN
Indiana, PA
Bridgeport, MI
Putney, KY
Dalton, GA
Villa Rica, GA
Crown Point, IN
Pensacola, FL
Knoxville, TN
Findlay, OH
Hammond, IN
Temperance, MI
Green Pond, AL

Gardendale, AL
Burlington, NC
Chattanooga, TN
Washington, IA
Chattanooga, TN
Hixson, TN
Claysburg, PA
Rossville, GA
Troy, MO
Haines City, FL
Pulaski, TN
Newark, CA
Resaca, GA
Louisville, KY
Winchester, KY
Rossville, GA
Warner Robins, GA
West Chester, OH
Winston-Salem, NC
Mount Airy, NC
Tampa, FL
Asheville, NC
Petersburg, IN
Tuscaloosa, AL
Ellisville, MS
Cleveland, OH
Pride, LA
Trenton, GA
Etowah, TN
Severn, MD
Thomasville, GA
Huntsville, Ontario,
  Canada
Toronto, Ontario,
  Canada
Valdosta, GA
Dayton, TN
Walkertown, NC
Goldsboro, NC
Bridgeport, WV
Santa Clara, CA
Greenville, NC
Chatsworth, GA

Blountsville, AL
Poplar Bluff, MO
Pinellas Park, FL
Aiken, SC
Akron, OH
Chattanooga, TN
St. Marys, WV
Adrian, MI
Dayton, OH
Columbia, MD
Belpre, OH
Oxford, PA
Brooklyn, NY
Orange Park, FL
Jamestown, NY
Chattanooga, TN
Trenton, GA
Greeneville, TN
Kendallville, IN
Phoenixville, PA
Anderson, IN
Resaca, GA
Inver Grove Heights,
  MN
Rosemount, MN
Golden Valley, MN
Fridley, MN
McLeansville, NC
Mocksville, NC
Rochester, NY
Sulphur, LA
Chattanooga, TN
Jupiter, FL
Oxford, AL
Chattanooga, TN

1991
Fayetteville, GA
Scottsboro, AL
South Boardman, MI
Fayetteville, NC
Pigeon Forge, TN
Manchester, TN

Panama City, FL
Morristown, TN
Murfreesboro, TN
Cuernavaca, Morelos,
    Mexico
Durham, NC
Walkertown, NC
Chattanooga, TN
Winston-Salem, NC
Newton, NC
Texas City, TX
Glendale, AZ
Covington, GA
Versailles, IN
Huntsville, AL
Hixson, TN
Statesville, NC
Lakeland, FL
Poland, OH
Garland, TX
Cleveland, TN
Chattanooga, TN
Ft. Oglethorpe, GA
Ballard, WV
Louisville, KY
Kernersville, NC
Clayton, IN
Crown Point, IN
Guin, AL
Douglasville, GA
Charlotte, NC
Memphis, TN
Kennesaw, GA
Delray Beach, FL
Chattanooga, TN
Panama City, FL
Martinsville, VA
Dalton, GA
San Leandro, CA
Lancaster, CA
LaGrange, GA
Athens, AL
Brookville, IN

Bridgeport, MI
Resaca, GA
Pikeville, TN
Chicago, IL
Rossville, GA
King, NC
Chattanooga, TN
Lake City, GA
Morrow, GA
Chickamauga, GA
Shelby, NC
Asheville, NC
Athens, AL
Loxley, AL
Bay Minette, AL
Ripley, WV
Trenton, GA
Scott Depot, WV
St. Albans, WV
Pocatalico, WV
St. Albans, WV
Scott Depot, WV
Selmer, TN
Greenwood, IN
Richmond, VA
Lexington, NC
Winston-Salem, NC
Trenton, GA
Winston-Salem, NC
South Pittsburg, TN
Winston-Salem, NC
Lawrenceville, GA
Sandston, VA
Prospect Heights, IL
Chattanooga, TN
Troy, AL
Stokesdale, NC
Mocksville, NC
Walkertown, NC
Chatsworth, GA
Decatur, GA
Estill Springs, TN
Adrian, MI

Millersburg, MI
Sulphur, LA
Carbon Hill, AL
Scottsboro, AL
Pelham, AL
Harriman, TN
Livonia, MI
Baton Rouge, LA
Arcola, LA
McLeansville, NC
Chillicothe, OH
Milford, OH
Resaca, GA
Bay Shore, NY
Crown Point, IN
Jacksonville, FL
Santa Maria, CA
Tampa, FL
Chattanooga, TN
Crab Orchard, WV
Harrison, TN
Tennessee Ridge, TN

1992
Erwin, TN
Maryville, TN
Calhoun, GA
Ft. Worth, TX
Mesquite, TX
Manchester, TN
Florence, AL
Bowling Green, KY
Ft. Oglethorpe, GA
Americus, GA
Beaver Dams, NY
Palmyra, NY
Piedmont, AL
Gadsden, AL
Lake Butler, FL
Natchez, MS
Gulfport, MS
Hattiesburg, MS
Blue Springs, MO

Newport News, VA
LaPlata, MD
Calvert City, KY
Lawrenceville, GA
Stone Mountain, GA
Charlotte Harbor, FL
Lakeland, FL
North Ft. Myers, FL
Fayetteville, NC
Albany, GA
Tallahassee, FL
Waterford, PA
Winter Haven, FL
Knoxville, TN
Chattanooga, TN
San Antonio, TX
Mission, TX
Osawatomie, KS
Terre Haute, IN
Powell, TN
Roanoke, VA
Crown Point, IN
Colonial Heights, VA
Englewood, TN
Torrington, CT
Temperance, MI
Hixson, TN
Jemison, AL
Knoxville, TN
Sacramento, CA
Chico, CA
Proctorville, OH
Clinton, MD
Carrollton, OH
Haines City, FL
Evansville, IN
Winston-Salem, NC
Yadkinville, NC
Murfreesboro, TN
Corpus Christi, TX
Dalton, GA
Murfreesboro, TN
Warren, OH

Irvine, CA
Pleasantville, IA
Resaca, GA
Asheville, NC
Escondido, CA
Mogadore, OH
Cahokia, IL
Trenton, GA
Mount Airy, NC
Nicholasville, KY
Silver Springs, FL
Waverly, TN
Etowah, TN
West Columbia, SC
Arnold, MO
West Union, WV
Chattanooga, TN
Chattanooga, TN
Pensacola, FL
Pulaski, TN
Perry, FL
Trenton, GA
Westminster, MD
Suwanee, GA
Pinellas Park, FL
Cape Coral, FL
Rosemount, MN
Chattanooga, TN
   (SWBF)
Crown Point, IN
Burbank, IL
Chattanooga, TN
Tampa, FL
Adrian, MI
Chickamauga, GA
Columbus, GA
Pineville, NC
Fayetteville, NC
Greensboro, NC
Calhoun, GA
Baton Rouge, LA
Belpre, OH
Elizabethton, TN

Greenville, NC
Circleville, OH
Belleville, MI
Resaca, GA
Milford, OH
Brewster, OH
Nicholasville, KY
Farmington Hills, MI
Chattanooga, TN
Harrison, TN
Rossville, GA
Dayton, TN

1993
Birmingham, AL
Dalton, GA
Burlington, NC
Tallahassee, FL
Crossville, TN
Williamsburg, KY
Cuernavaca, Mexico
Acapulco, Mexico
Jacksonville, FL
Chattanooga, TN
Meridian, MS
Gulfport, MS
Hattiesburg, MS
Stockton, CA
Lancaster, CA
Walkertown, NC
Panama City, FL
Harriman, TN
Crown Point, IN
Calvert City, KY
New Franklin, MO
Florence, AL
Valdosta, GA
Hooker, GA
Kingsport, TN
Spencer, WV
Elkview, WV
Sissonville, WV
Columbia, MD

Smyrna, TN
Temperance, MI
San Leandro, CA
Wendell, NC
Charlotte, NC
Louisville, KY
Colonial Heights, VA
Ragland, AL
Morrow, GA
LaGrange, GA
Longview, TX
Cleveland, VA
Ft. Worth, TX
Roanoke, VA
Jonesborough, TN
Stockbridge, GA
Dalton, GA
Louisville, KY
Winder, GA
Tifton, GA
Rockford, IL
Charlotte, NC
Fayetteville, GA
Dickson, TN
La Plata, MD
Bessemer, AL
Atoka, TN
Tuscaloosa, AL
Pineville, NC
Bay City, MI
Chickamauga, GA
Resaca, GA
Chattanooga, TN
Campbellsville, KY
Barstow, CA
Crossville, TN
Tallahassee, FL
Asheville, NC
Skyland, NC
Wallingford, CT
Trenton, GA
Harrison, TN
Chattanooga, TN

Bridgeport, MI
Walkertown, NC
LaFayette, GA
Trenton, GA
Jackson, MI
Athens, AL
Mocksville, NC
Pensacola, FL
Bay Minette, AL
Red Bank, TN
Graniteville, SC
Trenton, GA
Santa Clara, CA
San Antonio, TX
Beeville, TX
Dryden, Ontario,
    Canada
Etowah, TN
Barnesville, GA
Chattanooga, TN
Crown Point, IN
Rosemount, MN
Athens, AL
Canton, OH
Gallipolis Ferry, WV
Dalton, GA
East Ridge, TN
Lebanon, MO
Chattanooga, TN
Hazard, KY
Nicholasville, KY
Tallahassee, FL
Port Charlotte, FL
Chattanooga, TN
Portsmouth, VA
Resaca, GA
Rowlett, TX
Garland, TX
Chattanooga, TN
Cove, AR
Soddy Daisy, TN
Brooklyn, NY
Harrison, TN

Chattanooga, TN

1994
Monroe, NC
Gastonia, NC
Cape Coral, FL
Pinellas Park, FL
Jefferson, GA
Cuernavaca, Mexico
Oklahoma City, OK
Powell, TN
Rome, GA
Walkertown, NC
Chattanooga, TN
Newton, NC
Columbiana, OH
Calvert City, KY
Tupelo, MS
West Chester, OH
Charlotte Harbor, FL
Ft. Myers, FL
Georgetown, TN
Hurricane, WV
San Antonio, TX
Dunn, NC
Salem, VA
Dunnellon, FL
Rossville, GA
Niagara Falls, Ontario,
    Canada
Crown Point, IN
Florence, AL
Powell, TN
Churchville, MD
Greenville, SC
Elizabethton, TN
Matthews, NC
Stockbridge, GA
Temperance, MI
Wheaton, MD
Roanoke, VA
Powell, TN
Panama City, FL

Nashville, TN
Cahokia, IL
Tower Hill, IL
Hickory, NC
Chattanooga, TN
Lewisville, TX
Morristown, TN
Tunnel Hill, GA
Chattanooga, TN
Southington, CT
Dayton, TN
Brewer, ME
Versailles, IN
Ft. Oglethorpe, GA
Roswell, GA
Athens, AL
Athens, GA
Dalton, GA
Santa Clara, CA
Wildomar, CA
Moreno Valley, CA
Irvine, CA
Trenton, GA
Round Rock, TX
Walkertown, NC
Valdosta, GA
Scottsboro, AL
Madison, TN
Milan, TN
Hixson, TN
Tampa, FL
Brewster, OH
Indianapolis, IN
Trenton, GA
Whitwell, TN
Rockford, IL
Louisville, KY
Cahokia, IL
Charlotte, NC
Kokomo, IN
Nassau, Bahamas
Paterson, NJ
Stone Mountain, GA

Campbellsville, KY
Ironton, OH
Baton Rouge, LA
Monroe, NC
Adrian, MI
Hammond, IN
Mableton, GA
Hazard, KY
Statesville, NC
Milford, OH
Ft. Oglethorpe, GA
Harrison, TN
Chattanooga, TN
Crown Point, IN
Murfreesboro, TN
Fayetteville, NC
Henderson, KY
Soddy Daisy, TN
Hopkinsville, KY
Pride, LA
Harrison, TN

1995
Mocksville, NC
Stockbridge, GA
Manchester, TN
Jacksonville, FL
Boonsboro, MD
St. Croix, U.S. Virgin
    Islands
St. Thomas, U.S. Virgin
    Islands
Murray, KY
Oklahoma City, OK
Morrow, GA
Mexico City, Mexico
Athens, AL
Loxley, AL
Montgomery, AL
Winder, GA
Pinellas Park, FL
Chattanooga, TN
Hodgenville, KY

Ft. Pierce, FL
Temperance, MI
Lakeland, FL
Chattanooga, TN
Huntsville, AL
Crossville, TN
Hammond, IN
Harlan, IA
Morrisonville, IL
Jasonville, IN
Upper Marlboro, MD
Somerset, NJ
Pensacola, FL
De Soto, TX
Festus, MO
Louisville, KY
Crown Point, IN
Columbia, MD
Chattanooga, TN
Douglasville, GA
Garland, TX
Hudson Falls, NY
Lakeview, MI
Charlotte, NC
Rockmart, GA
Abingdon, VA
Charlotte, NC
Eros, LA
West Columbia, SC
Chattanooga, TN
Riverview, FL
Peoria, IL
Cumming, GA
Tallassee, AL
Dunlap, TN
Kansas City, KS
Santa Clara, CA
Chattanooga, TN
Burlington, NC
Charleston, WV
Bowling Green, KY
Lynchburg, VA
Lawrenceburg, IN

Chattanooga, TN
Ooltewah, TN
Tampa, FL
Winona Lake, IN
Ripley, WV
Mount Airy, NC
Rockford, IL
McComb, MS
Hinesville, GA
Raleigh, NC
Powell, TN
Taylors, SC
Richmond, VA
Massillon, OH
Covington, GA
Mount Olive, NC
Baltimore, MD
Hammond, IN
Chattanooga, TN
Trenton, GA
Lithia Springs, GA
Greenville, SC
Greenville, SC
Adrian, MI
Roanoke, VA
Statesville, NC
Oliver Springs, TN
Greenfield, IN
Monroe, NC
Milford, OH
Chesapeake, VA
Hazard, KY
Ft. Oglethorpe, GA
Acworth, GA
East Bethel, MN
Ashtabula, OH
Rock Hill, SC
Cleveland, OH
Crown Point, IN
Hammond, IN
Kokomo, IN
Paducah, KY
Clinton, MD

Akron, OH
Harrison, TN
Birmingham, AL

1996
Birmingham, AL
Mocksville, NC
Haines City, FL
Urbana, OH
Chattanooga, TN
Bowling Green, KY
Richardson, TX
Oklahoma City, OK
Walkertown, NC
Ft. Oglethorpe, GA
Knoxville, TN
Ringgold, GA
Scottsboro, AL
Hope, AR
Athens, AL
Hodgenville, KY
Jasonville, IN
Durham, NC
Brooklyn, NY
Louisville, KY
Williamsport, PA
St. Petersburg, FL
Ft. Pierce, FL
St. Louis, MO
LaFollette, TN
Indianapolis, IN
Morrisonville, IL
London, KY
Morrow, GA
Columbia, TN
Shelbyville, TN
Columbia, TN
Chesapeake, VA
Hammond, IN
Crown Point, IN
Jackson, MI
Montague, MI
East Ridge, TN

Winder, GA
Houston, TX
Great Falls, MT
Morganton, NC
Denham Springs, LA
Van Buren, OH
Tower Hill, IL
Centralia, IL
Godfrey, IL
LaFayette, GA
Springfield, TN
Chattanooga, TN
Mill Creek, WA
Versailles, IN
Lancaster, CA
San Francisco, CA
Meridian, MS
Lynchburg, VA
LaFollette, TN
Walkertown, NC
Walnut Cove, NC
Angola, IN
Indianapolis, IN
Dayton, TN
Bedford, VA
Dalton, GA
Columbus, GA
El Dorado, AR
Mocksville, NC
Athens, TN
Lexington, NC
Greenville, SC
Portsmouth, VA
Knoxville, TN
Chattanooga, TN
Spokane, WA
South Point, OH
Avon, IN
Jacksonville, FL
Casper, WY
Adrian, MI
Pinellas Park, FL
Baldwin, FL

Tunnel Hill, GA
Raleigh, NC
Crown Point, IN
Temperance, MI
Walkertown, NC
Milford, OH
Cincinnati, OH
Rossville, GA
Shreveport, LA
Indianapolis, IN
Little Hocking, OH
Kokomo, IN
Crown Point, IN
Soddy Daisy, TN
North Charleston, SC
Trenton, GA
Chattanooga, TN
Harrison, TN
Jonesboro, GA

1997
Macon, GA
Tampa, FL
Garland, TX
Manchester, TN
Stone Mountain, GA
Oklahoma City, OK
Signal Mountain, TN
Murfreesboro, TN
Walkertown, NC
Brooklyn, NY
Raleigh, NC
Clinton, MD
Newton, NC
Monroe, NC
Ringgold, GA
Memphis, TN
Santa Clara, CA
Jefferson, GA
Hammond, IN
Murfreesboro, TN
Rossville, GA
Dalton, GA

Chattanooga, TN
Decatur, IL
Roanoke, VA
Chattanooga, TN
Powell, TN
Ridgeway, VA
Lithia Springs, GA
Shreveport, LA
Chattanooga, TN
Independence, MO
Osawatomie, KS
Chattanooga, TN
Olathe, KS
Bonne Springs, KS
Lenoir City, TN
Richardson, TX
Sewanee, TN
Tupelo, MS
LaFollette, TN
Stockbridge, GA
Ocala, FL
Rossville, GA
West Salem, OH
Elyria, OH
Americus, GA
Birmingham, AL
Orange City, FL
Versailles, IN
East Ridge, TN
Oliver Springs, TN
Leesburg, VA
Angola, IN
Walkertown, NC
Mocksville, NC
Reidsville, NC
New Bloomfield, PA
Winston-Salem, NC
Trenton, GA
Winter Springs, FL
Rossville, GA
West Union, WV
Ft. Myers, FL
Fayetteville, NC

Valdosta, GA
Morristown, TN
Hammond, IN
Byron, GA
Stone Mountain, GA
Butler, PA
Springfield, TN
Chattanooga, TN
Hammond, IN
Cincinnati, OH
Lynchburg, VA
Athens, AL
Griffin, GA
Carbon Hill, AL
Milford, OH
Corydon, IN
Greensboro, NC
Kingsport, TN
Chattanooga, TN
South Point, OH
Chattanooga, TN
King, NC
Cleveland, TN
Baldwin, FL
Soddy Daisy, TN
Jacksonville, AR
Morrow, GA
Harrison, TN
Montgomery, AL
Orange Park, FL
Ellisville, MS
Columbus, GA
Dallas, TX
Chattanooga, TN
Covington, GA
Lakeland, FL
Trion, GA
Ringgold, GA
Kernersville, NC
Jonesboro, GA
Bucyrus, OH

1998
Oxford, AL
Mansfield, OH
Atco, NJ
Boonsboro, MD
Chattanooga, TN
Dothan, AL
Tampa, FL
South Pittsburg, TN
Powell, TN
Reidsville, NC
Elizabeth City, NC
Temperance, MI
Luzerne, MI
Chattanooga, TN
Dallas, NC
Chattanooga, TN
Williamstown, WV
Columbiana, OH
Signal Mountain, TN
Ellettsville, IN
Hammond, IN
Crown Point, IN
Haines City, FL
Mocksville, NC
Charleston, WV
Orion, MI
Statesville, NC
Soddy Daisy, TN
Hagerstown, MD
Arlington, TX
Stone Mountain, GA
Rockford, IL
Kenosha, WI
Powder Springs, GA
Adrian, MI
Chattanooga, TN
Soddy Daisy, TN
Charlotte, NC
Winder, GA
Fayetteville, GA
LaGrange, GA
Kittanning, PA

Orange City, FL
Rossville, GA
Athens, AL
Gardendale, AL
East Chicago, IN
Chattanooga, TN
Trenton, GA
Gaines, MI
Murfreesboro, TN
Walkertown, NC
Spring City, TN
Dalton, GA
Festus, MO
Trenton, GA
Soddy Daisy, TN
Covington, GA
Newton, NC
Morristown, TN
Hazard, KY
Pineville, NC
Terre Haute, IN
Monroe, NC
Albany, GA
Springfield, OH
Hartselle, AL
Durham, NC
Van Buren, OH
Winder, GA
Chattanooga, TN
Stone Mountain, GA
Penndel, PA
Summerville, GA
Chattanooga, TN
Marietta, OH
Cleveland, OH
Knoxville, TN
Ft. Oglethorpe, GA
Stony Brook, NY
Brooksville, FL
Etowah, TN
Columbus, GA
Bradenton, FL
Petersburg, IN

Richmond, VA
West Columbia, SC
Cincinnati, OH
Soddy Daisy, TN
Kokomo, IN
Harrison, TN
Williamston, SC